Integrating the National Science Education Standards into Classroom Practice

Kenneth P. King

Roosevelt University

Upper Saddle River, New Jersey
Columbus, Ohio

Library of Congress Cataloging-in-Publication Data

King, Kenneth P.
Integrating the national science education standards into classroom practice/Kenneth P. King
   p. cm.
Includes bibliographical references and index.
ISBN 0-13-117345-6 (alk. paper)
1. Science—Study and teaching—United States. 2. Education—Standards—United States. I. Title

LB1585.3.K56 2007
507.1′073—dc22   2006021777

Vice President and Executive Publisher: Jeffery W. Johnston
Associate Editor: Meredith Sarvar
Senior Editorial Assistant: Kathleen S. Burk
Production Editor: Alexandrina Benedicto Wolf
Production Coordination: Carlisle Publishing Services
Design Coordinator: Diane C. Lorenzo
Cover Designer: Jeff Vanik
Cover Image: Corbis
Production Manager: Pamela D. Bennett
Senior Marketing Manager: Darcy Betts Prybella
Marketing Coordinator: Brian Mounts

This book was set in Bookman by Carlisle Publishing Services. It was printed and bound by Command Web. The cover was printed by Phoenix Color Corp.

Pearson Prentice Hall™ is a trademark of Pearson Education, Inc.
Pearson® is a registered trademark of Pearson plc
Prentice Hall® is a registered trademark of Pearson Education, Inc.
Merrill® is a registered trademark of Pearson Education, Inc.

Pearson Education Ltd.   Pearson Education Australia Pty. Limited
Pearson Education Singapore Pte. Ltd.   Pearson Education North Asia Ltd.
Pearson Education Canada, Ltd.   Pearson Educación de Mexico, S.A. de C.V.
Pearson Education—Japan   Pearson Education Malaysia Pte. Ltd.

10 9 8 7 6 5 4 3 2 1
ISBN: 0-13-117345-6

Contents

PART 2
Programs and Policy

Special Features

Supporting Science Teaching Standards

Supporting Assessment Standards

Supporting Science Content Standards

Supporting Professional Development Standards

Preface

Integrating the National Science Education Standards into Classroom Practice offers preservice teachers—both secondary content specialists and elementary generalists—a tool to see not only *what* the National Science Education Standards are, but also *how* they can shape the practice of teachers.

The National Science Education Standards (NSES) serve as a means through which American educational systems can support effective science education programs for its children. The NSES have not been composed from the point of view that there is a single issue that must be "fixed" in order to produce scientifically literate citizens. Rather, a variety of issues, perspectives, programs, and a multitude of educational systems interact with each other to produce scientifically literate citizens.

The NSES operate from the point of view that students, teachers, and teacher educators must work together to produce effective programs that will help all students achieve their potential as thoughtful, participating citizens.

To prepare students to learn science—and to prepare other students to become effective teachers of science—some common ground needs to be established. The notion of achieving scientific literacy provides a helpful construct to organize instructional and teacher education practices. The National Science Education Standards provide that framework.

The NSES offer suggestions for preparing teachers, supporting inquiry-based practices for teaching and assessing science, and providing objectives for developing science education programs. For those interested in a map of content to be covered, I would recommend the American Association for the Advancement of Science's excellent *Benchmarks for Scientific Literacy* and *Atlas of Scientific Literacy*.

What Is the Approach for This Book?

I have had two distinct roles in science education: as a science teacher and as a science educator. My experiences as both a practitioner and professor of science pedagogy inform the vignettes that open each chapter. Each chapter begins with a snapshot of traditional teaching practices and then closes with descriptions of practices that emphasize the spirit of the National Science Education Standards.

For those who may see the materials in the standards as being theoretical, I can assert not only the value of what they offer to both preservice and practicing teachers, but how they offer a means of thinking about what it is to teach science. For experienced teachers, the closing chapters of this book examine their role in developing science curriculum and being part of a larger process to develop science experiences for their students—within an entire science education system.

The focus of the experiences is on science as it is taught from the intermediate grades through high school. Having spent the last year as a full-time public school teacher, I have strengthened my resolve to support more inquiry-based experiences, a greater variety of assessments for students, and the participation of teachers in the creation and implementation of their own professional development.

Throughout the text the standards will be carefully examined. Artifacts from my own experiences as a public school teacher and as a teacher educator are used to illustrate teaching, program development, and curricular practices, which will help the reader understand the science education goals, practices, and attitudes that comprise the NSES.

Theoretical/Conceptual Framework

As the tenth anniversary of the National Science Education Standards approaches, this book serves as a helpful reminder—or introduction for most preservice teachers—of the value and purpose of the standards.

The standards are organizational tools that inform science teaching practices. Most methods textbooks do an exemplary job of describing content and pedagogy and then connecting those issues with the standards. This text starts with the standards and then describes instructional/staff development/content-related practices within the context of the standards. As such, it may at times read like a methods book. At other times, it will help students develop an intellectual framework of *what* the standards are and how they can be used to develop their professional practice through teaching experiences and understanding the science education systems from K–16.

The key pedagogical features of each chapter are the opening and closing vignettes. The opening vignettes describe traditional practices associated with science teaching, such as direct instruction, one-shot staff development exercises, paper-and-pencil assessment practices, and the like. These are not "poor" teaching practices; they just represent very traditional practices. In most cases, these practices are familiar to students and are practices which they probably plan to emulate in their own classrooms.

Each chapter examines a specific standard and provides readers with an understanding of what it means in terms of teaching and learning. Along the way, exemplary activities are drawn from the literature and from my experience as a science teacher and as a teacher educator. The examples, ranging from connecting students with resources to sample activities, were selected to develop, in the most concrete manner possible, the elements of the standards and to help students perceive what they might look like in practice.

Each chapter closes with a vignette about teaching practices that are informed by the specific standard. As with the pedagogical examples embedded in the text, these closing vignettes are drawn from both the literature and my experiences. The goals are to show what standards-informed experiences look like in practice and to help readers see themselves in that role as they enter the teaching profession.

Overview of the Text

The National Science Education Standards address six broad areas related to creating and maintaining strong programs in science education from pre-K experiences through graduate school. This text examines each of the standards and seeks to operationalize them for classroom practice. Each chapter offers sample activities drawn from contemporary classroom practice that demonstrate the spirit of the NSES as they are put into practice.

Chapters 1 through 4 form Part 1 of the book and look at issues that are of the most immediate concern to new teachers: content, methods, and assessment. Chapter 1, Teaching for K–12 Scientific Literacy, introduces the inquiry approach as a means of teaching science and makes a case for the need to look at science as a continuous set of experiences.

Chapter 2, Standards for Science Teaching, provides background and justification for teaching science from a perspective that supports inquiry-based experiences.

Chapter 3, Standards for Assessment in Science Education, acknowledges that as the movement to support inquiry-based practices in science education has evolved, so to has the need for assessment practices that are consistent with inquiry-based experiences for students. It provides an overview of contemporary performance-based assessment practices.

Chapter 4, Standards for Science Content, stresses that the content knowledge associated with science is both an end in itself and a vehicle for students to learn process and problem-solving skills. This chapter examines how content knowledge is developed in an inquiry-driven classroom environment.

Part 2 looks at the broader program and policy issues that inform science teaching. Chapter 5 examines the standards for science education programs. A broad science program represents an interrelationship among science content, science curriculum, and assessment of science standards. Chapter 6 examines how these factors interact with each other and how they influence our teaching and other professional practices.

Chapter 6, Standards for Science Education Systems, examines the relationships among federal, state, and local systems that support science education. The chapter seeks to raise the reader's awareness of these systems and identify inservice and preservice practices that help to move these science education systems in a direction that is more compatible with inquiry-based experiences.

Chapter 7, Standards for Professional Development for Teachers of Science, emphasizes professional development as the key to high-quality, long-term professional practice that leads to personal satisfaction. It discusses the need for professional development and what it might look like when teachers work to design and implement their own professional development practices.

Chapter 8 reflects on the meaning of the standards for teaching science.

Acknowledgments

My gratitude to the kind people at Merrill/Prentice Hall is boundless. Their patience and encouragement are profoundly appreciated, especially when I returned to the public schools as a science teacher for a period of time and lost the luxury of writing during the workday that I had as a professor.

Linda Bishop and Allyson Sharp's talents of taking my rough ideas and helping to craft them into something more worthwhile helped me appreciate, more than ever, the value of the relationship between a writer and an empathetic editor. In addition, their patience with my progress—always moving ahead, albeit often very slowly—is appreciated on both a personal and professional level. Laura Weaver's consistently cheerful e-mail messages were always a bright spot in my day.

A number of individuals provided comprehensive and thoughtful feedback for this work. They improved both the readability and intellectual rigor of the text, and for their time and efforts, I extend my appreciation. My thanks go to C. David Christensen, University of Northern Iowa; Deborah J. Tippins, University of Georgia; Jose M. Rios, University of Washington, Tacoma; Kerri Skinner, University of Nebraska at Kearney; Margaret S. Carter, James Madison University; Mary Margaret Capraro, Texas A&M University; Michael Odell, University of Idaho; Michelle Scribner-Maclean, University of Massachusetts, Lowell; Robbie V. McCarty, Southwestern Oklahoma State University; Ross H. Nehm, The City University of New York; and Tom Roy, Marian College.

Gratitude and love, as always, to my family: Tina, my wife, and my sons Marshall and Harrison. Tina as a public school teacher and my sons as elementary students remind me always to ensure that science in the classroom is engaging, inspiring, and fun.

Teacher Preparation Classroom

TEACHER PREP

MERRILL
PRENTICE HALL

See a demo at
www.prenhall.com/teacherprep/demo

Your Class. Their Careers. Our Future. Will your students be prepared?

We invite you to explore our new, innovative and engaging website and all that it has to offer you, your course, and tomorrow's educators! Organized around the major courses pre-service teachers take, the Teacher Preparation site provides media, student/teacher artifacts, strategies, research articles, and other resources to equip your students with the quality tools needed to excel in their courses and prepare them for their first classroom.

This ultimate on-line education resource is available at no cost, when packaged with a Merrill text, and will provide you and your students access to:

Online Video Library. More than 150 video clips—each tied to a course topic and framed by learning goals and Praxis-type questions— capture real teachers and students working in real classrooms, as well as in-depth interviews with both students and educators.

Student and Teacher Artifacts. More than 200 student and teacher classroom artifacts—each tied to a course topic and framed by learning goals and application questions—provide a wealth of materials and experiences to help make your study to become a professional teacher more concrete and hands-on.

Research Articles. Over 500 articles from ASCD's renowned journal *Educational Leadership*. The site also includes Research Navigator, a searchable database of additional educational journals.

Teaching Strategies. Over 500 strategies and lesson plans for you to use when you become a practicing professional.

Licensure and Career Tools. Resources devoted to helping you pass your licensure exam; learn standards, law, and public policies; plan a teaching portfolio; and succeed in your first year of teaching.

How to ORDER *Teacher Prep* for you and your students:
For students to receive a *Teacher Prep* Access Code with this text, instructors **must** provide a special value pack ISBN number on their textbook order form. To receive this special ISBN, please email **Merrill.marketing@pearsoned.com** and provide the following information:
- Name and Affiliation
- Author/Title/Edition of Merrill text

Upon ordering *Teacher Prep* for their students, instructors will be given a lifetime *Teacher Prep* Access Code.

Science Teaching, Science Content, and Assessment

Part 1 of this book—Chapters 1, 2, 3, and 4—examines issues of great importance to new science teachers: teaching through inquiry, developing meaningful assessment practices, and understanding the scope and breadth of science content.

For those who are beginning their careers in education, it is a chance to examine the practice of inquiry in science teaching, and how it compares to more traditional practices that you have experienced as a student. For those who have more experience as a teacher and assessor of learning, the first part of this book will provide a benchmark for inquiry-based teaching practices and performance-based assessments supported by the *National Science Education Standards*.

CHAPTER 1

Teaching for K–12 Scientific Literacy

CLASSROOM SNAPSHOTS

Jennifer had played school for as long as she could remember. First she had lined up her dolls in neat rows in her playroom, and then she cheerfully coerced her younger brothers and sisters to participate in her schoolhouse role plays. She graded pretend papers, she read books to her real and imaginary students, and she stood at her chalkboard and showed how to make perfectly formed Zaner-Blosser letters.

Now she was one semester away from student teaching and one year away from having her own classroom full of eager and enthusiastic students. With the start of the new fall semester, she was enrolled in her professional education coursework. Reading methods and language arts methods were the courses that she had expected, but with her college's redesign of the elementary education program, she now had to take a course in the methods of teaching science. A vague sense of alarm washed through Jennifer. This was not something she had role-played with her dolls and siblings years before.

Entering the cheerfully decorated science methods classroom helped a bit. The professor had arranged the classroom to look much like a well-equipped elementary classroom, but with adult-sized furniture. After an opening activity involving milk, dishwashing detergent, and food coloring, Jennifer found herself most intrigued. The food coloring created fascinating patterns in the milk when a drop of detergent was added to the pie pan of milk. This was not science as she had remembered it.

After the activity and some time spent exploring the concepts developed through the activity, class discussion turned to the course syllabus and the required materials for the course. Again, the experience was different from other science-related courses she had taken, as the instructor did not require any books of the sort that she was familiar with. One book that Dr. Rojo held up was the National Science Education Standards. See the *Try This!* 1–1 activity for an activity that introduces inquiry to younger children.

Jennifer could barely suppress the moan that was welling up inside of her. "Science education standards?" she said to herself, "all I want is some good activities to share with my students next year. How is reading a book on science standards going to help me to do that?"

 Try This! 1–1 *Introducing Inquiry to Intermediate Children*

Materials needed for pairs of students:

- Cup of milk
- Four different colors of food coloring
- Several brands of dishwashing detergent
- Aluminum pie pan
- One small vial or container
- Clear Pyrex-type pie pan

For a follow-up activity:

- Water in a clear glass
- Pepper

Procedure

Give each group an aluminum pie pan and a vial of detergent. Do not disclose that the vials contain detergent. Let the students infer what the liquid is from their observations. You might wish to call it "mystery liquid" to challenge them and provoke some questions.

Ask them to pour one cup of milk into the pie plate. Have each child choose one color of food coloring, and place one drop near the perimeter of the pan. To involve all students, you might wish to have each student be responsible for a specific color. Some interesting results might appear at this point—for example, the size of the drops will likely be the same from the droppers of food coloring, but the sizes of the drops may appear to be different when placed in the milk. Often, these apparent differences are caused by the greater density of one color of food coloring—they might sink to the bottom! This would be a great chance to challenge a child to offer an explanation; be ready with a clear pie pan so they can test their explanation. Note, however, that developmentally, understanding the concept of density is more appropriate for older students.

After the food coloring is placed in the milk, a student should place a few drops of detergent on the lip of the pie plate, allowing it to run into the milk. Suddenly, when the detergent reaches the milk, an amazing mixing of the colors will take place. As the students watch the explosion of colors, have them make observations. Drawing pictures is a great way for younger students to record their observations, so be ready with crayons or markers and paper.

Each child should have an opportunity to put detergent into the milk throughout the activity. Some may prefer to place it directly on the swirling colors. After the activity is ended, discuss the children's observations. Ask them what they think the yellow liquid is. Help students understand why we use detergents and soaps to clean things.

To help clarify their understanding, ask your students to lightly sprinkle pepper—so it floats—on the surface of a clear glass of water. Ask, "What can you do to sink the pepper?" [Use detergent to break the cohesive attraction forces of the water molecules that form a film on the surface and sink the pepper.]

The Science Content

The molecules of the milk form a thin skin on its surface called surface tension. This is what allows water skimmers (insects) to scurry across the surface of a body of water. The detergent destroys the connections between the water molecules at the surface of the milk, allowing the food coloring to move freely through it (remember that milk is made up mainly of water). This reaction helps explain why we use detergents and soaps with water to clean things. Having the food coloring float on the surface of the milk helps to provide evidence for the changes the students produced in the surface tension of the milk.

How might you use this activity to get students to ask questions about what is taking place?

How might you use this activity to get students to find the means to answer the questions they developed?

What role should the teacher take during this investigation?

Introduction

What are the National Science Education Standards?

Professor Robert Yager (2003) of the University of Iowa introduced a recent discussion on the National Science Education Standards by noting that they were produced at a cost of some seven million dollars—which works out to over $26,700 per page. "What," he inquired, "makes this document worth the investment of our tax dollars?"

The National Science Education Standards have the simple objective of helping to achieve scientific literacy for members of our society. While the goal is simple and straightforward, the challenges associated with implementing that goal are profound.

To begin with, there are a variety of definitions of what constitutes scientific literacy. Bybee (1997) does an admirable job of synthesizing the various definitions, slogans, perspectives, and purposes ascribed to the goal of producing scientifically literate students and citizens. For this volume, the definition of scientific literacy reported in the National Science Education Standards will provide the direction and purpose for teaching science in elementary and secondary schools.

> Scientific literacy is the knowledge and understanding of scientific concepts and processes required for personal decision making, participation in civic and cultural affairs, and economic productivity. It also includes specific types of abilities. In the National Science Education Standards, the content standards define scientific literacy. (National Research Council, 1996, p. 22)

The definition of scientific literacy has a strong element of social action built into the concept. While *science* literacy focuses on the mastery of content knowledge, *scientific* literacy focuses on using that knowledge to achieve social good. The connection to the broader community and how to use the information for social good is an important part of the broader aims of education in

America—producing participating citizens. Science–Technology–Society perspectives on instruction, as you will see in subsequence chapters, likewise seek to promote and institutionalize this element of social action as a part of the learning experience. The perspective taken in the National Science Education Standards also supports this position.

CLASSROOM SNAPSHOTS

Late in his junior year in college, chemistry major Benjamin slipped into his science teaching methods course. He smiled to himself as he thought about how he would finally be teaching next year. All he really worried about was whether he knew enough chemistry to teach well and how to get his students to behave once he started teaching. His own high school chemistry class, taught by Mrs. Lobo, still inspired him. Hopefully he would be able to teach his students and inspire them in the same way that she had inspired him to love chemistry and then to want to teach it himself.

In the meantime, he had to make it through his methods course. "Methods of teaching science?" he wondered to himself. "What I really want is to learn some more demonstrations—like the time Mrs. Lobo put the flower into the liquid nitrogen and it shattered. Now that was great teaching!" See *Implementation Idea* (Lesson 1.1) for one way you might consider implementing a short-term inquiry experience with real data for secondary students.

SUPPORTING SCIENCE TEACHING STANDARD: LESSON 1.1

Implementation Idea: Short-Term Inquiry—Secondary Level

Using the 2002 edition of the *Wisconsin Endangered Resources Report*, Bunton (2003) noted that the data describing the population of wolves in the state of Wisconsin was showing a transition from the introduction of the new species to one reflecting the beginning of exponential growth. This behavior is due to the population of wolves having been nearly decimated in the recent past, so that its current population trends more nearly resembles that of a newly introduced species to an area.

To help students begin developing their own questions that would lead to student-directed inquiry, Bunton helped them confirm what they knew about changes in populations, helped them focus and develop what they suspected to be true, and then helped them understand whether or not they needed answers to questions such as:

- What does the wolves' food web look like?
- What does the deer population curve look like?
- What changes in deer population can be anticipated as a result of the appearance of chronic wasting disease?
- If there is a change in the deer population, what effect will this have on the wolf population?
- What are the dependent and independent limiting factors for the wolf? (p. 42)

These questions led to a long-term investigation into wolves in particular and, through the study of wolves and the changes associated with their population, helped students learn more about using real data to answer their own questions. While Bunton concedes that not as much content knowledge was covered by this approach, as compared to a more didactic approach, the enhanced data collection and analysis led his students to a depth of understanding he had not previously encountered during his tenure as a classroom teacher.

(Adapted from Bunton [2003], "Predicting Population Curves").

Benjamin's reflections were interrupted by his professor calling the class to order. After a brief round of introductions, Dr. Milson moved the class into the laboratory to start the course off with an activity. Ben was intrigued by the investigation, which started with a real-world question regarding changes in wolf population levels in the state of Wisconsin. Though Benjamin was majoring in chemistry, he hoped to teach biology as well; he found the questions Dr. Milson posed intriguing. The follow-up discussion by Dr. Milson helped Benjamin understand how much of what he learned—and still wanted to learn—about the population changes among wolves was generated by his own questions. Benjamin was further intrigued by the possibilities of using real data and inquiry. He still hoped that he would learn some cool demonstrations, but he was awakened to some possibilities that had heretofore remained dormant—that he could help students really "do" science by encouraging inquiry in the classroom.

It is hoped that you will see some of your experiences in each of the vignettes presented, whether you are planning a career as an elementary, middle school, or secondary teacher. While many methods books are written for a grade-specific audience, the Standards are written from the point of view that all meaningful science experiences have much in common and that the continuum of experiences in science education are best delivered by teachers who not only know what experiences their students have had before they reach their classroom, but also what sort of experiences will prepare their students for the next science class they will take and how they will use that knowledge as participating citizens. Indeed, in my own experiences as a teacher educator, [I have found that the most meaningful experiences for students come from courses that enrolled both elementary and secondary students.] [The power of the experiences for my students in that setting is evident in that elementary teachers learn as much from secondary teachers as secondary teachers learn from their colleagues in the elementary grades.]

The interaction of elementary science teachers with secondary science teachers helps each group appreciate the cognitive transitions and growth in knowledge students will experience—and can serve to make them more insightful teachers of their current group of students. Students—whose teachers understand the structure and organization of science teaching as a discipline—benefit from teachers who perceive the big picture and can help them engage in science learning experiences that will help them to become more successful, autonomous problem solvers as they experience their school system's science curriculum.

It is important to see the opportunities available to you as you take on the rewarding challenges of teaching science in a way that supports student inquiry, problem solving, and finding the answers to questions in concert with your students. It is hoped that you will see yourself in the "post standards" vignette, at the close of each of the following chapters as you begin developing and implementing your own set of skills that support effective science teaching consistent with the National Science Education Standards (NSES).

Defining and Debating Inquiry

As you will discover in the chapters that follow, the changing emphases in instruction, program, and assessment suggested by NSES were created to promote the notion of *inquiry* in science teaching. For the moment, however let us examine in detail what inquiry means in the context of science teaching.

Inquiry is the prevalent theme of the National Science Education Standards. This theme has become more widespread in teacher-preparation programs, and much of the current science education research seeks to define what inquiry is, what it looks like in the classroom, and how teachers may increase their success in implementing inquiry-based experiences for their students.

Rankin (2000) offers this insightful description for inquiry:

> Inquiry in hands-on learning is often distinguished by the amount of flexibility a teacher allows in order for children to develop individual curiosity and ways to solve problems. This is different from a situation in which a teacher poses a question and then directs all the students to take the same pathway to find a common solution. In case of inquiry, the teacher may have a very good idea of what scientific concepts he would like the children to learn, but he allows for a lot of variation in the children's investigations, recognizing that there may be many solutions to the same problem. (p. 35)

One caution about the term "inquiry": it is used to describe a wide assortment of science teaching practices (Kluger-Bell, 2000). Various experiences—guided discovery activity, a learning-cycle structured lesson, an open-inquiry lesson—represent different facets of inquiry.

> Good science inquiry involves learning through direct interaction with materials and phenomena. One important sign of inquiry is the relative level of control that the students have in determining various aspects of the learning experience. (Kluger-Bell, 2000, p. 47)

In general, the more direct experience students have with materials, the better. However, in an era when the mantra of "hands-on" is used to bless the "best" science experiences, the root of inquiry comes from how the students guide their own explorations and generate and seek to solve the questions that develop during their investigations. The classic Elementary Science Study (ESS) program has its foundation in open-inquiry experiences that lead students of all ages to ask and answer their own questions, leading to a deeper and more profound construction of their own understanding. Review the science investigation in Try This! 1–2 to see a remarkable series of activities that help students engage in productive and meaningful scientific inquiry.

 Try This! 1–2 *Structures: Instructional Highlights for Investigations*

Materials (vary depending on activities the student performs)

- 250g modeling clay per student
- soft drink straws (allow about 100 per student)
- 500 straight pins
- 50 index cards
- 500 paper clips
- cardboard tubes
- glue
- 100 large washers
- 1″ × 2″ wooden strips, holes drilled through ends
- bolts and wing nuts (to fasten wooden strips together)

Building with Clay

Problem for students: How large or tall can a structure be formed with modeling clay? Note how students, who generally have experience with modeling compounds, intuitively construct objects with the clay. Use a meter stick to measure structures to sustain interest. Pose divergent and convergent questions to encourage the students to interact with the material and to challenge and deepen their understanding of what makes objects stand. Further challenges to pose to students: *Could you make a structure twice as tall with twice as much clay?* (p. 15)

Another extension might be to ask students to use what they have learned about building modeling clay towers.

Straws and Pins

In the straws-and-pins activity, students are again given open-ended challenges to construct freestanding structures such as towers using straws and pins. As with the clay construction activity, circulate among the students to evaluate their problem solving strategies and further challenge them by asking them to compare their work with their neighbors, by challenging them to construct a tower of the same height using fewer straws, and by having them explain how what they learned during the clay-construction activity applies to building structures with straws.

Challenge students further: *How can you test your structures for strength, for stability, and for durability? How are their structures similar to structures that might be encountered outside the classroom? What patterns do you notice that are common to the tallest structures? Do structures that were built as towers work equally well as bridges?* (p. 22)

One of the notable patterns that will emerge from these manipulations is that successful towers tend to have broad bases as well as having noticeable cross-pieces or braces that support the structure. Ask students how these elements influence the way the structure stands and how these factors relate to increasing the height of the structure.

Paper Tubes and Index Cards

The patterns that emerged from the construction activities using the straws and modeling clay are now tested and expanded through construction activities that feature paper tubes and index cards. Challenging questions to pose to students include: *How strong can you make a piece of ordinary writing paper? How can it be rolled or folded to increase the load that it will support?* (p. 29) Seek out similarities between what made successful structures with straws and pins and what made for successful structures with paper tubes and index cards.

Large-scale Structures

As a culminating activity, building large-scale structures with $1'' \times 2''$ strips of wood (fastened together with bolts and wing nuts) can be most instructive. Apply the principles derived from the previous investigations to the construction of large-scale structures. The application of concepts related to effective structures takes on new significance when students are able to climb on or across structures that they have constructed themselves.

Adapted from *Teacher's Guide for Structures* (Elementary Science Study, 1970).

What Do the Standards Offer Us as Preservice and Practicing Teachers?

As prospective teachers, the NSES offers first and foremost a broad perspective on the structure and importance of science education for America's schools. They ask teachers and future teachers to appreciate science as more than just a content-specific body of knowledge. Science education is a progressive program of developing knowledge and problem solving skills that thrive in an atmosphere of student-driven inquiry.

In addition, the Standards provide us an opportunity to see science education as a set of complementary strands of experience, including not only content knowledge but also practices that support effective assessment and professional development of teachers, both at the preservice and inservice levels of professional practice.

The Standards are also designed to help teachers develop an appropriate knowledge of what combination of experiences support teaching science as inquiry. Developing a more informed notion of what practices are consistent with inquiry is essential. Change statement in question to read: "Learning how to use assessment as a guide for effective inquiry-based instruction is another theme present in the Standards. Planning for assessment and instruction at the same time helps the teacher to better understand what he or she is teaching by determining at the same time how to assess the student's growing knowledge.

Knowledge of the NSES will also help you to recognize how to serve as an advocate for exemplary science education practices. Understanding the value of science teaching and understanding what structures need to be in place to support effective science teaching require support on a number of levels, from high-level policy makers to classroom teachers. Working to support good science teaching at all levels serves to undergird the belief that scientific literacy is an important goal for all of our citizens.

Summary

Expect this book to help you see how the National Science Education Standards serve as a framework for the practices you will engage in as a science teacher. Use the vignettes in the classroom snapshots as reference points for practices that are consistently well-thought-out, but, in the case of the NSES-informed practices, represent experiences that are part of a broader pedagogy that supports inquiry for the children you will teach.

References

Bunton, M. (2003). Predicting population curves. *The Science Teacher, 70*(4), 41–44.

Bybee, R. W. (1997). *Achieving scientific literacy*. Portsmouth, NH: Heineman.

Elementary Science Study. (1970). *Teacher's guide for structures*. New York: McGraw-Hill.

Kluger-Bell, B. (2000). Recognizing inquiry: Comparing three hands-on teaching techniques. *Foundations, 2*, 39–50.

National Research Council (1996). National Science Education Standards. Washington, DC: National Academy Press.

Rankin, L. (2000). Lessons learned: Addressing common misconceptions about inquiry. *Foundations, 2*, 33–38.

Yager, R. E. (2003). *Curriculum Discussion: The National Science Education Standards*. Presentation at the annual meeting of the National Association for Science Technology and Society, Baltimore, MD.

CHAPTER 2

Standards for Science Teaching

CLASSROOM SNAPSHOTS

It's 7:40 A.M. The final bell for first period rings and a flurry of students pass through the doorway to room 153. The class is well-ordered, quiet, and businesslike. Mr. Pink, the teacher, has already placed an overhead transparency on the overhead projector, noting upcoming events in the life of his physics students. Besides listing discussion topics for the day's lecture, the notes also give due dates for upcoming assignments and the upcoming unit exam on force and motion. A few students groan as they think about one of Mr. Pink's famously difficult multiple-choice physics tests.

Students pull out their homework papers from the previous day's assignment, and the teacher collects the materials from them for grading that evening. After the assignments are collected, he offers solutions to a few of the more challenging problems and offers a perfunctory "any questions?" query to the class. There being no questions, Mr. Pink pulls out another overhead transparency sheet from the manila folder on his desk and launches into a presentation on how equations of motion are derived to describe acceleration. He offers a few sample problems, checks students for their understanding by asking questions during his presentation, and then asks his students to try a problem independently. Mr. Pink circulates around the room, offering feedback and helpful commentary as individual students try the equations out, following the model offered by the teacher.

Halfway through the class period, Mr. Pink wheels an apparatus from the back corner of the room and performs a demonstration showing how to measure the acceleration of a falling body. The demonstration confirms, with few discrepancies, the equations of motion he presented during the first half of class. He notes that the following class period will be used as a laboratory period, during which the class will confirm the equations of motion they developed in class using materials similar to the one Mr. Pink just demonstrated.

The demonstration completed, Mr. Pink gives the class the remaining minutes of class to begin work on the homework assignment. He circulates, as before, checking on student progress. Students continue quietly working until the moments before the bell signaling the passing time between periods 1 and 2. Mr. Pink wishes his students well, sends them off to their next class, and rearranges his notes and his demonstration to use with his second period physics students.

Introduction

Perhaps you saw in the preceding classroom scenario some elements of your life as a high school student. It should be emphasized that there is *nothing wrong* with the classroom experience shared above. Much good teaching and learning can—and has—taken place in a traditional classroom. The point that will be developed throughout this book is that traditional, teacher-centered, curriculum-focused, large-group instruction is only a *part* of the experience of teaching science. A broader and more comprehensive set of experiences for students is the challenge offered by the contents and implications of the National Science Education Standards (NSES). Effective teaching of science, as outlined in the NSES, seeks to move the students to more overt acts of scientific inquiry. Traditional large-group teaching and learning settings work well for communicating large blocks of content information. The goal, however, of the NSES is to work on developing depth in student learning, as opposed to practices that focus on increasing breadth of learning. The core of learning should come from student-generated questions that lead students to actually engage in inquiry. As we examine the changing emphases for science education standards, it will become clear that the commitment to teach science becomes more of a commitment to learn *with* students as students pursue answers to questions. The teacher seeks to help students find their own answers through their own knowledge, skills, training, and pedagogical and personal insights.

Changing Emphases for Science Education Standards

The table below offers a clear statement of the direction current practices in science education should move in order to become more student-centered and more inquiry-centered. Compare the elements of Table 2.1 with the teaching vignette at the beginning of this chapter and the teacher-directed nature of that classroom. The teacher in the Classroom Snapshot is teaching in a very traditional manner, with all of the elements for teaching success in place: he communicates his goals to his students, he offers an organized presentation with opportunities for guided and independent practice, and he gives students feedback via his review of the homework assignments.

The setting described above is helpful for students if the science goal is to engage students in mastering content knowledge. However, teaching science—and learning science—is a more complicated and richer task than simply amassing factual knowledge. The heart of science, as is emphasized in the NSES, is the acquisition of knowledge through student-generated questions. The content of Table 2.1 underscores this perspective.

TABLE 2.1   Changing Emphases for Science Education Standards*

Less Emphasis On	More Emphasis On
Treating all students alike and responding to the group as a whole	Understanding and responding to individual student's interests, strengths, experiences, and needs
Rigidly following curriculum	Selecting and adapting curriculum
Focusing on student acquisition of information	Focusing on student understanding and use of scientific knowledge, ideas, and inquiry processes
Presenting scientific knowledge through lecture, text, and demonstration	Guiding students in active and extended scientific inquiry
Asking for recitation of acquired knowledge	Providing opportunities for scientific discussion and debate among students
Testing students for factual information at the end of the unit or chapter	Continuously assessing student understanding
Maintaining responsibility and authority	Sharing responsibility for learning with students
Supporting competition	Supporting a classroom community with cooperation, shared responsibility, and respect
Working alone	Working with other teachers to enhance the science program

*Reprinted with permission from *National Science Education Standards* © 1966 by the National Academy of Sciences, courtesy of the National Academies Press, Washington, D.C. p. 52.

Scientific inquiry as an instructional goal is the point of view supported by the National Science Education Standards, the National Science Teachers Association, and the American Association for the Advancement of Science. As a methodology and as a philosophy, there is abundant research support for teaching science in this manner. There are, however, perceived obstacles to teaching through inquiry. These issues will be addressed throughout the remainder of the text, but let this list serve to alert the reader as to what he or she should be looking for, especially if you can identify with one or more of the perceived obstacles to practice.

Lack of Resources: The belief—and often the reality—that the school and the individual classroom lack necessary resources to teach science through inquiry is one of the key issues.

Standardized Assessment: In an era during which teacher and student accountability remains an issue, addressing this important concern is paramount.

Teacher Content Knowledge: The teacher's perceived lack of content knowledge can place well-meaning teachers at a disadvantage, as their willingness to enter into an instructional "unknown" often means that science is among the least taught of all the disciplines.

Pedagogical Concerns: If content knowledge represents the "what" of science teaching, pedagogical concerns represent the "how" of teaching. Teachers, both novice and experienced, often have questions as to what teaching with a focus on inquiry looks like in the classroom.

Classroom Management: This represents a specific issue under the general concept of pedagogy. Managing students is always a concern, but managing students as they individually explore their own questions creates an instructional environment that offers different management concerns than a standard direct instruction lesson.

The change in orientation for the science teaching standards underscores several key instructional points. First and foremost, the use of inquiry as the primary focus of classroom experiences is emphasized. To this end, the teacher and his or her students *share* the learning experiences rather than having them dictated to the students by the teacher. Etheredge and Rudnitsky (2003) note the following essential elements for scientific inquiry to be present in the classroom. In all cases, be aware of the emphasis on problem solving within each of these steps.

Problem sensing: A discrepant event or incongruity stimulates awareness of a problem, as can an observation, an intriguing idea, or a real-life issue.

Problem formation: An attempt is made to define or clarify the problem.

Searching: Questions about the problem are raised, information is gathered, hypotheses are formulated, and alternative solutions are explored.

Problem resolving: The incongruity is removed to the satisfaction of the learner. (p. 10)

These elements of problem solving are also consistent with lesson plan models, such as the learning cycle and its components of exploration, engagement, explanation, and extension. Problem sensing can be correlated with the *engagement* phase of the lesson, during which the students are challenged with a problem or given a discrepant event to consider, engaging their interest in the knowledge to be gained.

Problem formation helps students to *explore* new problems by working together with other students. The discussion and joint analysis of the problem helps them to construct their own understanding of the problem they wish to investigate. Searching continues the *explanation* phase of the lesson, as students seek to formulate their hypotheses and prepare to test their understanding in new circumstances, *extending* their understanding. Try This! 2–1 Discrepant Event would be useful in provoking a discussion regarding properties of matter.

 ## Try This! 2–1   *Discrepant Event*

A variation on a traditional teaching strategy is the *discovery demonstration*. In this approach, the teacher silently conducts a demonstration while the students try to determine what is taking place. Students are typically allowed to ask questions that may be answered by the teacher either stating "yes" or "no" (Wolfinger, 1984).

Show students two identical 250 ml graduated cylinders. Add one drop of food coloring to each cylinder. Encourage student questions about the purpose of the food coloring and other tasks that they observe (the food coloring makes the liquids easier to see).

Add 100 ml of water to one graduated cylinder and 100 ml of rubbing alcohol to the second. Move the cylinders closer to the students and allow them to confirm that each cylinder holds 100 ml of liquid.

Add the contents of one cylinder to the other. Swirl the cylinder to mix the liquids well. Show the graduated cylinder containing both liquids to students: the volume will be slightly less than 200 ml. At this point, encourage further questions regarding why this might have taken place.

Interpretation: Relative to alcohol, water has a rather "open" structure that allows alcohol to "fill in" the interstices between the water molecules. As such, the sum of the volume of the two liquids is slightly less than what most students would predict. As an example of a discrepant event, it promotes equilibration and results in cognitive disequilibrium. With the guidance of the teacher, the experience can be enlightening and will help students make sense of their observations.

Helpful in using discrepant events is a model proposed by Friedl (1986). In this model, there are three basic steps:

1. set up the event; confront students with the experience
2. engage students in dealing with the event
3. resolve questions and relate the event to scientific knowledge

Problem resolving confirms the new knowledge for the student. He or she should now be able to extend their understanding to new situations and be able to draw generalizations from their experience.

This instructional approach assumes that the students are conversant with and can apply science process skills. The "classic" process skills, identified and used to provide the foundation for the American Association for the Advancement of Science's *Science: A Process Approach* curriculum include the following: observing, classifying, measuring, communicating, inferring, predicting, using space/time relationships, using numbers, formulating hypotheses, making operational definitions, experimenting, and interpreting data (AAAS, 1967).

Moreover, all of these elements of inquiry are consistent with the standards set forth in the NSES. Whether the inquiry is short term and focused on a single discrepant event or long term with a potential resolution still weeks away, the movement toward scientific inquiry forms the foundation of the NSES.

Examining and Interpreting the Science Teaching Standards

The National Science Education Standards document outlines what has come to be considered the best teaching practices in science for an inquiry-driven experience. Beyond the changing emphases in classroom practice discussed above, there are specific sets of standards that relate to the teaching of science. The teaching standards are designed to support practices in curriculum development, student discourse, performance-based assessment and metacognitive skills, and a coherent and well-articulated science program.

Science Teaching Standard A

Science Teaching Standard A seeks to assist teachers in developing a curriculum and set of experiences that promotes scientific inquiry. Inquiry is one of the essential experiences for students learning science and can too easily be neglected in favor of marching through more content knowledge. Clearly, content knowledge is essential, and this goal is supported by other science standards. A comprehensive science experience, however, blends mastery of content knowledge with the application of process skills, while delving into scientific inquiry.

Implementing Science Teaching Standard A in the classroom continues to provide a challenge for teachers. Textbooks have dictated curriculum for years, and moving from using the book as an instructional outline to an instructional resource is a transition that will not be made lightly. Moving from a curricular

---

SCIENCE TEACHING STANDARD A

Teachers of science plan an inquiry-based science program for their students. In doing this, teachers

- Develop a framework of yearlong and short-term goals for students.
- Select science content and adapt and design curricula to meet the interests, knowledge, understanding, abilities, and experiences of students.
- Select teaching and assessment strategies that support the development of student understanding and nurture a community of science learners.
- Work together as colleagues within and across disciplines and grade levels.

philosophy of perennialism (knowledge as unchanging truths) and essentialism (focus on proven knowledge) dictated by textbooks to perspectives informed by elements of progressivism and reconstructionism (both of which consider knowledge to be ever-changing and individually constructed) is a major paradigm shift for many teachers (Passe, 1999).

The challenge to be embraced here is that the process of inquiry promotes the acquisition of new knowledge in ways that complement the curriculum and students' interests. The challenge of meeting the needs of students and the needs of the curriculum have been issues that educators have struggled with for a long time. The classic text, John Dewey's (1902) *The Child and the Curriculum,* underscores the call to address both the needs of the student and the broader needs of comprehensive knowledge development. With respect to teaching and learning science, Dewey offered these thoughts:

> The third evil is that even the most scientific matter, arranged in logical fashion, loses this [vital and organic] quality, when presented in external, ready-made fashion, by the time it gets to the child. It has to undergo some modification in order to shut out some phases too hard to grasp, and to reduce some of the attendant difficulties. What happens? Those things which are most significant to the scientific man, and most valuable in the logic of actual inquiry and classification, drop out. The really thought-provoking character is obscured, and the organizing function disappears. Or, as we commonly say, the child's reasoning powers, the faculty of abstraction and generalization, are not adequately developed. (p. 204).

While our goals have broadened beyond preparing the "scientific man" to preparing boys and girls with a modicum of scientific literacy, the challenges of ensuring that the needs of the child and the curriculum are met are addressed in tandem; that is, the instructional needs of the child are recognized and met, while at the same time ensuring the curriculum is delivered in a meaningful and cogent fashion.

Science Teaching Standard B

The role of the science teacher shifts dramatically in the NSES-oriented classroom. Teaching Standard B emphasizes the role of the teacher as one of modeling inquiry and facilitation, rather than the more common incarnation as dispenser of factual knowledge. Looking back to the vignette that opened this chapter, none of these elements were present. The teacher organized his classroom to help students amass a set of discrete content knowledge. Rather than using inquiry as the operating principle, he sought to ensure that students could acquire and apply the information he shared with them independently. The interaction stopped well short of promoting inquiry through student-generated questions.

The sort of interaction favored by Mr. Pink included checking students' understanding. This is a valuable strategy. Checking for understanding allows teachers to gain insight into what a student is learning and how it is being organized into their existing schema, that is, how individuals cognitively organize information and use that organizational approach to engage in future learning. This traditional classroom methodology provides opportunities for higher-order questions to emerge, but as presented, this instructional approach had no means for students developing, engaging, and answering their own questions. Rather, the focus was on

---

SCIENCE TEACHING STANDARD B

Teachers of science guide and facilitate learning. In doing this, teachers

- Focus and support inquiries while interacting with students.
- Orchestrate discourse among students about scientific ideas.
- Challenge students to accept and share responsibility for their own learning.
- Recognize and respond to student diversity and encourage all students to participate fully in science learning.
- Encourage and model the skills of scientific inquiry, as well as the curiosity, openness to new ideas and data, and skepticism that characterize science.

acquiring knowledge that the teacher set forth during the lecture and demonstration. Students would have to "buy into" Mr. Pink's planned lesson goals to own any learning. And, as you may have experienced yourself, unless students become intrinsically motivated to learn, they may not get engaged in a lesson.

The chance to engage in science as "argument and explanation" is likewise missing from Mr. Pink's lesson. While there were some discrepancies between the predicted data points and the actual data points collected during the demonstration, they were brushed aside as being incidental to the instructional points Pink was making. Rather than use the discrepancies as an opportunity for deeper investigation and exploration, they were characterized as "incorrect" results. As an example, the discrepancy between the predicted value and the measured value may relate to the force of friction that is produced as various parts of the experimental apparatus rub against each other. If Mr. Pink had allowed students to carry out the investigation themselves, it would have led to an opportunity for discovery among the students. As they compared their results with each other and discussed among themselves the difference between the predicted and measured results, Mr. Pink could use their discoveries to not only make his desired instructional point about acceleration, but to also help students to learn more about forces by having them measure them and sort out the meaning through discussion and thoughtful teacher feedback. Review the lesson model profiled in Lesson 2.1 to get a sense of what inquiry might look like in an intermediate elementary classroom.

SUPPORTING SCIENCE TEACHING STANDARD B: LESSON 2.1

Curriculum Idea: Scientific Discourse

Oobleck is a substance made from cornstarch, water, and (in this instance) green food coloring. It has the curious property of behaving like a solid when pressure is applied to it and like a liquid when the pressure is removed. It is an excellent material for students to investigate properties of matter and to learn to defend their description of Oobleck's behavior through the use of their observations and data collection. Sneider's *Oobleck* does an excellent job of preparing students for a scientific convention during which they argue and debate the properties of Oobleck they have discovered. An adaptation of a lesson is presented below.

Engage

Set the scene for Oobleck: tell students that a spacecraft has returned from another planet. This planet is covered with large, green oceans, and a sample of the ocean material was collected. It has been named "Oobleck" since it resembles the substance in the book *Bartholomew and the Oobleck* (Seuss, 1949). Tell students that preliminary studies have shown that Oobleck is safe to handle.

Exploration

Ask students to investigate the properties of Oobleck by using all of their senses, save that of taste. As the students explore the properties of Oobleck, they should record their findings. One student is assigned the task of recorder and should record the findings on a large sheet of paper, so that they can be later posted for all to observe and discuss. After the completion of a comprehensive list, have the students mark with a star the property of Oobleck that they found most intriguing.

Explain

Students should post their list of Oobleck's characteristics on the walls around the classroom. A point of debate will likely emerge among the starred items. Some students will attribute the change in Oobleck's behavior from solid to liquid as being due to

(continued)

providing pressure or force; others will deduce that the change in property is due to the addition of heat and warmth provided by their hands. Encourage debate and discussion on this point, and encourage students to explain their position and use their observations to support their position. Students should also be asked to diplomatically challenge the interpretations of other groups of students and how they used their observations to support a point of view. As a goal, it is desirable to come to a consensus on five or six generally agreed upon properties of Oobleck.

Reflection

The idea of science as "argument and explanation" is well-developed in the lesson plan profiled here. The possibility of misidentifying the cause for the property change, as well as justifying the position they took on other properties, gives elementary students the opportunity to challenge others' thinking, justify the answers they obtained using data, and develop new investigations to test the various interpretations being advanced during the students' scientific convention.

Adapted and modified from the Great Explorations in Math and Science (GEMS) teacher's guide entitled *Oobleck: What Do Scientists Do?* Copyright by The Regents of the University of California.

By putting the students in charge of their own learning experiences, the teacher opens up the curriculum to student interests. Finding ways to have students evaluate their own learning against a standard they set puts more of the responsibility in the hands of the student. Involving all students in a meaningful way is at the heart of teaching by inquiry and is universally advocated by science education professional organizations.

As demonstrated in Lesson 2.1, students have the opportunity to examine a variety of Oobleck's properties, and to use the observations they made to infer the properties of Oobleck. The classroom discussion allows students to consider multiple interpretations of the same data and to make judgments as to the best interpretation of the class' observations. In a similar way to Lesson 2.1, Lesson 2.2 provides a means for students to look for patterns in data sets. Examining the pattern in the data points that emerges provides one way of helping students to see the relationship between variables that they encounter during their science investigations.

SUPPORTING SCIENCE TEACHING STANDARD B: LESSON 2.2

Curriculum Idea: Data Analysis

Here's one approach that might be taken to examine the relationship between variables. The teacher can state in advance the connection between variables, but in this example, the teacher provided a data set and asked her students to decide which of the data sets produced a direct relation between the variables. This can be used to provide a foundation for understanding the relationships between the variables.

Problem

A graph that produces a straight line indicates a direct relationship between two variables. Use the information in the table below to determine the nature of the relationship between gravitational force (F, measured in newtons) and the distance between two objects (d, measured in meters).

Suggested Approach

Plot the data included below in four different ways:

- F as a function of d
- F as a function of d^2
- F as a function of d^{-1}
- F as a function of d^{-2}

If any of your data generates a straight line, calculate the slope of the line. What might this represent? What are the units for the slope of this line?

Force (N)	Distance (m)	Distance^2 (m^2)	1/Distance (1/m)	1/Distance^2 (1/m^2)
1.0	1.0			
0.25	2.0			
0.11	3.0			
0.063	4.0			
0.040	5.0			
1.0	1.0			

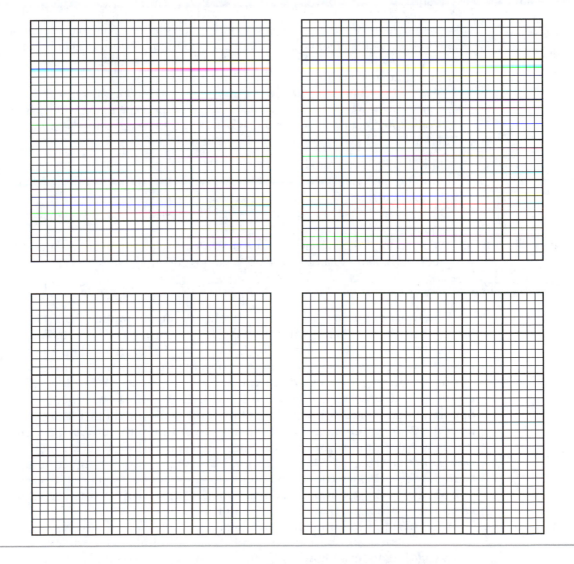

Meeting the needs of all students in science encouraged the American Association for the Advancement of Science (1989) to title their key reform document *Science for All Americans*. To this end, it must be recognized that not all students come to a classroom with either the same skills or the same life goals and interests. Students who want to be engineers, architects, and scientists clearly have a need to know and understand the processes of science; so do students who will have careers as artists, bankers, and bakers. But students often do not see the relevance of science in their lives or how owning science knowledge can impact their future as an adult. Using student-directed inquiry represents the primary challenge of creating a classroom that genuinely meets the needs of all students, preparing all students for their vocations and their everyday science needs.

The process skills of science include making use of data and drawing inferences from student-generated data. In this way, teachers help students to apply the skills of scientific inquiry. The example shown in Lesson 2.3 makes use of a well known, but often misunderstood example: the phases of the moon as observed from earth.

SUPPORTING SCIENCE TEACHING STANDARD B: LESSON 2.3

Process Skills and Meeting the Needs of All Students

Most people do not understand one of the most basic visions in the night sky: the phases of the moon. In a microcosm, understanding how an observer may make sense of the phases of the moon and from them infer the relationship between the earth, sun, and moon has many parallels in developing a scientific understanding of events. Tonight, write down the time that the moon rises. In addition, jot down a number of beliefs you have about the relationship between the earth, sun, and moon. Based on tonight's observation, make a prediction as to what time you expect the moon will rise tomorrow.

If you carried out this investigation as part of your science methods course, what did you find out?

1. How close was your prediction?
2. How does knowing [this] give you some insights into the value of data when trying to explain the behavior of a system such as the earth, sun, and moon?
3. Did your prediction fit into your existing belief system about the earth, sun, and moon?
4. What did this brief experience tell you about the relationship between observations, predictions, and explaining your observations and predictions?

The work of Marion, Hewson, Tabachnick, and Blomker (1999) is appropriate to note here. Their examinations of conceptual changes in students are relevant to the activity described in [Lesson 2.3.] In essence, a conceptual change paradigm creates opportunities for students to "synthesize models in their minds, beginning with existing explanatory frameworks" (Suping, 2003, paragraph 9). The process described in the activity requires that the teacher create opportunities for the student to identify and confront their initial conceptions, help the student create a new conception, and help the student accommodate the new information into an existing intellectual framework (Posner, Strike, Hewson & Gertzog, in Suping, 2003). This model of teaching through conceptual change provides the intellectual core for teaching science through inquiry or from a constructivist perspective. Look for those elements as you examine the various classroom activities profiled in this book.

Encouraging skepticism is not necessarily valued in a lesson such as the one that opened the chapter. Skepticism invites challenge and debate, whereas following the model laid out by the teacher encourages other traits, such as passivity and seeing the teacher as the font of all wisdom and knowledge. Our information-driven age requires not only access to knowledge, but also the skills to evaluate the quality of information. When the classroom genuinely values open dialog and challenging ideas, then it is clear that it is a place where open inquiry has a home.

SUPPORTING SCIENCE TEACHING STANDARD B: CURRICULUM IDEA 2.1

Connecting Science to Student's Lives—The Science of Automobiles

This list is certainly not comprehensive, but there are a multitude of science and technology concepts related to the operation of an automobile that connect the lives of students to material examined in science class.

- Friction between tires and road
- Incline of on ramps/off ramps and maximum safe speed for vehicles on ramps
- Changes in kinetic energy as car moves faster
- Inertia and the role of safety belts
- Light and optics: headlights
- Electricity: the electrical system of a car
- Simple machines embedded in the engine and body of an automobile
- Energy conversion (fuel to kinetic energy)
- Efficiency of engines and machines
- Energy and fuel conservation

Something for the reader to consider: does a theme such as this present a bias against girls? How can one ensure that topics do not perpetuate stereotypes?

Science Teaching Standard C

Assessment of student learning, as construed in Science Teaching Standard C, looks at assessment as a multifaceted experience. Mr. Pink's famously difficult multiple-choice examinations can be part of the entire assessment profile, but this kind of exam should not be used exclusively as a measure of student learning. A variety of assessment tools can and should inform the teacher of what the student knows, how well he or she knows the information or skill, and to encourage the teacher to use that information to organize instructional activities to better meet students' needs.

SCIENCE TEACHING STANDARD C

Teachers of science engage in ongoing assessment of their teaching and of student learning. In doing this, teachers

- Use multiple methods and systematically gather data about students understanding and ability.
- Analyze assessment data to guide teaching.
- Guide students in self-assessment.
- Use student data, observations of teaching, and interactions with colleagues to reflect on and improve teaching practice.
- Use student data, observations of teaching, and interactions with colleagues to report student achievement and opportunities to learn to students, teachers, parents, policy makers, and the general public.

The direction that teaching and learning is headed falls into the area of authentic assessment. When assessment is "authentic," it emphasizes the use of "assessment tools that more accurately mirror and measure what we value in education" (Hart, 1994, p. 9). Helping to align what is taught, what we want students to be able to do, and how we assess them seems to be the stuff of common sense. If we want students to actually be able to measure items, we ask them to *measure* the dimensions of an object; we would not ask them to answer questions about *how to measure* the dimensions of an object.

Referring back to the Oobleck investigation, one can see that there are many opportunities to assess what students have learned in an "authentic" fashion. As students debate the different models they have proposed for describing the behavior of Oobleck, teachers have the opportunity to see how students use data to develop explanations and models, as well as the quality of their reasoning. The final element of the Oobleck activity, in which students design spacecraft to land on a planet whose surface is covered with an ocean of Oobleck, gives the astute teacher insights into how students use information to solve problems—in this case, how they design a spacecraft to negotiate a green and sticky terrain.

SUPPORTING SCIENCE TEACHING STANDARD C: LESSON 2.4

Assessment Idea: Student and Teacher Crafted Rubrics

The following rubrics were developed by a secondary science teacher for a group of students who were carrying out a science inquiry project. As the investigations were quite open-ended, the teacher allowed the students to have input into the rubrics that were to be used to assess their work. The teacher gave each student a rubric with an empty grid, asking students to determine the weight of each category and the descriptions for each level of performance in each category. Two samples are included: the original document and a student-created model that was used to assess a student's project.

Weight	Element	Level 1 (1 point)	Level 2 (2 points)	Level 3 (3 points)	Level 4 (4 points)
	Planning				
	Research				
	Demonstration of Learning				
	Artifact/Product				
		No demonstration	Minimal demonstration	Extensive	Complete and compelling

It was not determined in advance by the teacher what the students would use to demonstrate the knowledge they acquired, so the "artifact/product" category ranged from poster presentations to videotapes to demonstrations of a project to a traditional paper describing what they learned during their investigation.

Weight	Element	Level 1 (1 point)	Level 2 (2 points)	Level 3 (3 points)	Level 4 (4 points)
20%	Planning	No planning evident	Plan created with appropriate deadlines; deadlines missed	Plan created with appropriate deadlines; deadlines mostly met	Plan created and implemented; deadlines consistently met
20%	Research	No sources cited	1–2 sources cited	3–5 sources cited, including primary documents	6–8 sources cited, all from primary sources
30%	Demonstration of Learning	Unclear	Student identifies some things that they learned	Student identifies what they learned and how it connects to the research they carried out	Student identifies what they learned, connects with the research they carried out, and identifies further areas for investigation
30%	Artifact/Product	Missing or sloppy	Minimally represents what was learned	Represents what was learned and the research they carried out	Represents what they learned, the research they carried out, and areas for future investigation
		No Demonstration	Minimal Demonstration	Extensive	Complete and compelling

Student-developed rubrics varied in terms of weighting the various elements of the rubric (within a range given by the teacher). Other rubrics reflected differences in the type of artifact that was produced and what constituted appropriate craftsmanship in its execution.

Using student feedback to guide teaching—formative assessment—is an essential part of developing more authentic assessments for students and teachers. Making use of student answers to questions moves the information gathered beyond letter grades. Using student answers to identify what they know—and possibly how well we teach—is the purpose that assessment should serve.

Also, helping students engage in assessing their own understanding promotes autonomous learning and assists them in understanding the value of learning. Promoting lifelong learning is included in the mission statement of nearly every school in the country. Helping students appreciate and then evaluate the quality of the information they have learned is more likely to have an effect on learning when students are encouraged to "own" the responsibility for their learning.

Just as we would have the students improve their ability to learn science, it is incumbent upon the teacher to learn how to *teach* science more effectively. Using data derived from student scores, from observations of other teachers at work, and from being observed by colleagues are among the first steps to moving a teacher from being a good teacher to a more effective one. Building a community of learners extends to the teaching staff as well as to the students in the classroom.

Science Teaching Standard D

Managing time, space, and resources is a responsibility of all teachers. There is no such thing as opening up a box that contains a perfect science lesson. For instance, the perception that the "perfect video" for a science classroom lasts 48 minutes out of the 50 allotted minutes to teach science is as erroneous as the idea that classroom investigations need to fit compactly into a 40- or 50-minute class period. Many—perhaps most—investigations that relate to student-generated inquiry will take longer than a single 50-minute class period to complete.

The challenge the teacher faces is to find ways to encourage and support long-term inquiry. Many of these issues are beyond the direct influence of the classroom teacher, for example, financial resources to acquire equipment or logistical issues such as class schedules. The teacher's role, however, is to lobby for increasing resources to create more flexible scheduling arrangements and convince administrators and others who control the purse strings and scheduling software to use their influence to support real inquiry in science teaching. Well-spent science monies can buy better equipment for inquiry. An appreciation for the value of science helps as scheduling decisions are made. Teachers, however, must be well-informed and plan carefully before requesting allocations to support a well-stocked inquiry classroom.

Within a single classroom, there is much that an individual teacher can do to support inquiry needs and develop deeper inquiry among his or her students.

> **SCIENCE TEACHING STANDARD D**
>
> Teachers of science design and manage learning environments that provide students with the time, space, and resources needed for learning science. In doing this, teachers
>
> - Structure the time available so that students are able to engage in extended investigations.
> - Create a setting for student work that is flexible and supportive of science inquiry.
> - Ensure a safe working environment.
> - Make the available science tools, materials, media, and technological resources accessible to students.
> - Identify and use resources outside the school.
> - Engage students in designing the learning environment.

Students need to be able to work in groups of varying size, depending on the project, to store materials, and to display and share their results as they move through their investigations (National Research Council, 1996).

To take one example, a middle school class examining factors that effect the growth of plants will probably work in small groups to research how variables effect plant growth, individually as they plant and grow their own plants, and then again in larger groups as they seek trends in how a variable produced differences in how the plants grew. Room for the plants to germinate and grow, whether on windowsills or on a plant stand, is only part of the space required for the investigation. Students' data and record keeping, whether through digital pictures or sketches of growing plants, also require storage space.

Safety in the classroom is paramount. Teachers and students need to ensure that inquiry is conducted safely, carefully, and with no risk to life or injury. Eye protection such as safety goggles, to cite one simple possibility, is as much a part of the tools of inquiry as test tubes, beakers, and Bunsen burners. Figure 2.1 offers a more comprehensive list of safety concerns for science classrooms.

Just as teachers need to help students engage in self-assessment, they also need to help students learn and understand how to work safely and how to anticipate and minimize risks in their investigations and their use of materials. Both schools and science teachers have an obligation to ensure that there is safe storage for materials and supplies and that safety devices, such as fire blankets and eye wash stations, are set up and in good repair.

FIGURE 2.1
Safety rules in the science classroom.

Supports SCIENCE TEACHING STANDARD D

Safety in the science classroom is essential. Rules for science safety may generally fall into three categories:

1. Rules required by legislation and school policy
2. Rules designed to support your classroom and activities
3. Rules appropriate for the maturity of your students.

Your primary concern, of course, is to ensure that students are safe and secure in the classroom, regardless of the source of the rules. One strategy to get student investment and compliance in classroom rules was reported by Davidson (1999). Davidson identified a number of key rules that may work for your own classroom. The strategy she suggests is to develop a contract that the student and parents both sign, signaling a commitment to following classroom safety rules. Among the key rules Davidson identified:

1. Safety goggles must be worn and be of the accepted type
2. Chemicals must be secured against unauthorized student use
3. Chemicals must be correctly labeled
4. Laboratory experiences must take place in the presence of the classroom teacher
5. Implementation of safe working conditions are the responsibility of the teacher and the school
6. The availability of appropriate materials is the responsibility of the school and their use is implemented by the teacher
7. Alcohol burners, which are susceptible to spills, are not recommended
8. Teachers must instruct students how to safely use all laboratory materials
9. "Teachers should be able to explain any explosion that takes place." (Davidson, 1999, p. 38)

Additional science classroom safety information is available online from the Council of State Science Supervisors, available at http://csss.enc.org/.

Other materials—beyond safety and scheduling needs—are also important in the pursuit of scientific investigations. Resources, such as computers, software, and the Internet, are part of contemporary working conditions and are the work tools students use as they engage in their investigations. Media, such as digital cameras, videotapes, and microcomputer-based peripherals, also need to be available to students to conduct data collection and analysis.

SUPPORTING SCIENCE TEACHING STANDARD D: CURRICULUM IDEA 2.2

Valuable Instructional Technology for Students

While this list cannot hope to be comprehensive—technology evolves at a staggering rate—these represent a few tools that teachers find helpful in connecting their students with both technology and learning.

Computer

- Internet connection
- Video projector (to share information with entire class)
- Scanner
- Printer
- DVD drive (a DVD drive in a computer can help the computer deliver information to students that once would have required a separate DVD player)
- Video camera
- Digital camera

Software

- Word processing
- Spreadsheets
- Presentation software
- Other specific software that has proven helpful:
  - *Inspiration*
  - *Kid Pix*
  - *Hyperstudio*
  - *Graph Club*
  - *Web-authoring software*
  - *Logo*
  - *Logger Pro*

Peripheral Devices (a few among many)

- *Accelerometers*
- *Light sensors*
- *pH sensor*
- *Voltage/current probes*
- *Magnetic field sensor*
- *EKG sensor*
- *Photogate*
- *Motion sensor*

Personal Digital Assistants

- PDAs now have a variety of peripheral sensors, allowing a lower cost alternative to computers for classroom data collection and analysis

SUPPORTING SCIENCE TEACHING STANDARD D: LESSON 2.5

Curriculum Idea: Using Technology and Resources Beyond the Classroom

The activities profiled in *Project Storm Front* show one way in which telecommunications technology can support science teaching in the middle school. Students in three separate sites in Illinois (one located on the shore of Lake Michigan, one located thirty miles west of the lake, and a third site located sixty miles west of the lake) collected weather data using simple equipment over a ten-week period of time. The proximity of one of the sites allowed students to speculate as to the influence of a large body of water on local weather conditions.

During the data collection phase, students had different roles each day as part of the science lesson. Some students collected data, others posted the information to the Internet, while still others began to look for patterns in the temperature, humidity, cloud cover, and other variables that correlated with the weather systems moving through the area. In that way, the presence of a single computer was not an obstacle to the learning; the teacher structured the activities so that all students participated in all phases of the project. Long-term inquiry and collaboration among different groups of students at different grade levels was also an advantage of this project.

Reflection on the Activity: This activity represents, as stated above, an opportunity to make use of resources beyond the classroom as well as an opportunity to conduct more extended inquiry. Data collected over a ten-week period at three different sites is never "tidy" in the manner of data provided in a textbook or lab book. Students engaged in this experience not only gathered information collaboratively, but they also had the opportunity to compare results and interpretations via e-mail-based discussions. Electronic resources, such as weather forecasting Web sites, and "rawer" data, such as satellite cloud cover photographs, helped to enrich the experience for the students at these sites.

Reprinted with permission from *Science Scope*, a publication of the National Science Teachers Association for middle level science teachers. Adapted from *Science Scope* article, "Tech Trek: Project Storm Front" (Thompson & King, 1998).

Resources also extend beyond the classroom walls as experts in many fields are available to help students in their investigations, whether they are interviewed by students after school hours, visit during the school day, or correspond with students via e-mail. One stellar example of this sort of experience is Project GLOBE. GLOBE helps students interact with professional scientists by encouraging them to

- Take scientifically valid measurements in the fields of atmosphere, hydrology, soils, and land cover/phenology, depending upon their local curricula
- Report their data through the Internet
- Create maps and graphs on the free interactive Web site to analyze data sets
- Collaborate with scientists and other GLOBE students around the world (GLOBE, paragraph 2)

More information about the exciting possibilities offered through GLOBE is available at http://www.globe.gov.

While activities such as Project GLOBE have a national and international reach, students can and should be involved in creating and contributing to their own learning environment. This involvement cultivates independence, and independence cultivates greater responsibility and autonomy among students.

Science Teaching Standard E

Teaching Standard E represents the framework within which teaching and learning science takes place. The program that teachers plan, develop, and implement determines in large part the experiences that their students will engage in. Too many teachers were handed a textbook before they began their career as a teacher and were told, "Here—this is your curriculum." Thoughtfully planning student learning experiences is a task that requires more deliberation than selecting pages from a school district course guide or the adopted school textbook.

Teachers also have an obligation to thoughtfully plan and develop a school's science program. To do this well, teachers need to understand that the curriculum they develop is part of a larger state, national, and international framework. Sadly, though many teachers take on this challenge, it is largely not supported with the time and resources necessary to plan effectively. But it can be done. Conscientious and effective teachers do it all the time. The activities you plan and the problem sets you assign should be meaningful for student learning.

> **SCIENCE TEACHING STANDARD E**
>
> Teachers of science actively participate in the ongoing planning and development of the school science program. In doing this, teachers
>
> ■ Plan and develop the school science program.
> ■ Participate in decisions concerning the allocation of time and other resources to the science program.
> ■ Participate fully in planning and implementing professional growth and development strategies for themselves and their colleagues.

Related to planning for effective science teaching, it is most advantageous if teachers are fully allowed to participate in the planning associated with how the school day is structured and how instructional resources are allocated. Teachers involved in curriculum planning and its implementation require that they have some involvement in how the school day is configured. Presently, most teachers have little control over these issues. This is an area where teacher advocacy should lay the groundwork for future professional preparation.

Professional growth for science teachers is the final challenge identified by Teaching Standard E. Far too often, staff development is something that teachers are subjected to and may be delivered to support administrative convenience rather than an experience designed to support effective science teaching. The professional development of teachers is far too serious a task to leave to happenstance. Professional development needs to be planned, implemented, and evaluated—along with the teacher's participation in the planning and implementation. Just as the standards recognize that the science curriculum should meet the needs of the students, as opposed to forcing a static curriculum on students, so too do teachers need to have their staff development experiences complement their knowledge, skills, and needs for growth. Staff developers informed of your needs can better meet them.

Scholarly Support for Standards and Teaching Through Inquiry

The major points in this chapter are related to the development and implementation of inquiry-based instruction in the science classroom. There has been abundant research over the last decade supporting the teaching of science through an inquiry-rich perspective. Schneider, Krajcik and Blumenfeld (in press) support the points made in this text as well: for teachers to be successful in teaching through inquiry, they must be prepared pedagogically, in terms of content knowledge, and in terms of sufficient resources to implement instruction through inquiry. When these elements are in place, learning has a greater likelihood of success. Lending further support for the likelihood of success in inquiry, based classrooms is the expectation that meaningful staff development experiences for teachers are required to effect change and that the process must be meaningful and long-lasting (Supovitz & Turner, 2000). A sobering realization further noted by Supovitz and Turner is that change in the schools is strongly related to the dominant socioeconomic status of the school, which has a greater effect on the success of transforming a school than does the inquiry-based program advocated by teachers and administrators. Clearly, if science is to be an endeavor for *all* children, then recognizing the challenges in place and working to overcome them becomes part of the "marching orders" for every committed classroom teacher. Despite the challenges noted above, high quality, *standards-informed* professional development practices can and do make a difference for preparing teachers to help students learn science through inquiry (Kahle, Meece, & Scantlebury, 2000). Together, these points alert the reader to the challenge and, ultimately, to the potential for success that awaits all teachers.

Implications for Practice

The challenge for preservice teachers is to transcend the experiences they have had as students and embrace the challenges of teaching science in a manner consistent with the NSES. This is a tremendous challenge. We all tend to teach in the same manner in which we were taught. Listening to lectures, taking notes, and watching demonstrations was the environment in which we were successful, and departing from that instructional culture is a great challenge.

CLASSROOM SNAPSHOTS

A National Science Education Standards-Informed Classroom
The bell rings at 7:40, but most students are already present and at work in Mr. Dreyer's earth science class. The topic of investigation for the quarter is groundwater contamination, and the students are looking into the impact of a proposed quarry on the community's water source. On the chalkboard, a student-written note serves to remind the members of the class that a group of students is scheduled to make a presentation to the city council during the month of April and that everyone's attendance and participation is expected.

Mr. Dreyer circulates around the room, checking on student progress suggesting the names of people and agencies to contact as resources, and offering ideas to pursue as students investigate their questions. One conversation evolves into a brainstorming session over organizations to contact, and, at the end of the session, plans are made to contact the county conservation service for information on drinking water and aquifers in the area.

Another group of students has completed their proposal to take a field trip to a construction site. They have arranged for the class to tour a mineral springs site in their county. They want to follow up on some evidence they have uncovered that changes in the water table can produce changes in natural springs, with hot springs and geysers being especially vulnerable. They are concerned that this local landmark might be susceptible to changes that could come about as a result of the excavation of the proposed quarry.

Reflecting back on the previous semester, Mr. Dreyer noted that the students were progressing in the curriculum at a pace that matched his expectations. He reflected on his initial apprehension and his students' apprehension when they started engaging in science experiences in problem-based learning and investigations in real issues. During a previous semester his earth science class developed an earthquake protocol for their school. The students were surprised to uncover the potential impact of the New Madrid fault on their school and community. They learned that while an event was unlikely, they were unprepared to deal with such an occurrence within their school. Students learned that geologic structures associated with earthquakes can have a social outcome, as buildings the way that people live are forced to adapt to the threat of earthquakes–and geologic features provide the clue used by community planners and builders. During that investigation, they consulted with experts ranging from other teachers to structural engineers and architects on the West Coast they had contacted through the Internet and e-mail resources. Also important was the impact of the information they learned from experts and consultants beyond their classroom walls.

As he made the rounds of his classroom, Mr. Dreyer thought back to the goals his students had set at the beginning of the quarter and how they were progressing toward them. Grading was certainly more challenging than giving students a set of multiple-choice exam questions, but the challenges were met with the rewards of helping students set their own goals and achieve them. Success was more than academic—it was personal.

The science classroom profiled here is not an example of "hopeful fiction." The examples taken from Mr. Dreyer's classroom are real activities done in a real classroom by an actual teacher named Mr. Dreyer. The real Mr. Dreyer teaches in this fashion, in a problem-based learning context, using real problems that were studied using questions students in his class developed, as opposed to the well-organized and well-practiced direct instruction model favored by Mr. Pink. The goals of the National Science Education Standards form the instructional basis for the classroom experiences he created. As we move through the rest of this book, we will make frequent comparisons between traditional classrooms and classrooms whose practices are informed by the NSES. While good teaching can take place in either classroom, more effective opportunities for learning are found in the student-centered classroom advocated in the Standards.

Summary

The focus of this chapter has been to explore the meaning of teaching through inquiry in the science classroom. The opening vignette presented a traditional, teacher driven and directed classroom experience. In concert with the National Science Education Standards, various elements of an inquiry-oriented classroom were examined, using classroom examples to demonstrate what the standards look like when they become part of classroom practice. The closing vignette profiles a classroom where inquiry is the primary instructional methodology and shows how students may learn rich content knowledge through student-directed inquiry.

- ■ Science education is currently in a time of transition as the development of the National Science Education Standards a decade ago help educators to reassess and reevaluate their teaching practices, their assessment practices, their approach to professional development, and their approach to science teaching from a perspective that embraces an inquiry-based approach.

- Traditional teaching practices, often through a direct instruction approach, can be honored and applied as part of a commitment to teaching science through inquiry, in concert with student's questions and the teacher serving as a mentor for the processes of *doing* science as opposed to a dispenser of scientific content knowledge.

- Instruction should work toward a goal of responding to individual student's interests and questions, rather than focusing exclusively on whole-class instructional practices.

- Rather than slavishly following a curriculum, recognize and use the curriculum as a set of guidelines that can be explored through student-directed inquiry and problem-based learning.

- Move away from a primary emphasis of focusing on student acquisition of discrete pieces of information to an instructional method that approaches science from a perspective that honors and supports student-generated inquiry as well as acquiring specific content knowledge—through application of problem solving and knowledge of process skills.

- Move away from teacher-directed approaches to delivering information in the form of lectures, texts, and demonstrations to instructional approaches that require students to engage in investigations supported by long-term inquiry.

- Embrace practices in teaching and learning that require students to use, explain, and defend how they have developed their knowledge and how they acquired and constructed their understanding of it.

- Develop thoughtful assessment practices that capture evidence of how students engage in the practice of science as well as the mastery and acquisition of content knowledge, and do this through continuous and ongoing student assessment.

- Develop and promote instructional practices that move to reconceive the teacher as a collaborator and fellow knowledge-builder, rather than as the ultimate classroom authority on what constitutes scientific knowledge.

- Move from a classroom environment that supports constant competition for grades to an environment in which students and teachers collaborate in the acquisition and development of new knowledge.

- Have teachers work together as professional colleagues in support of program development and professional development, rather than working in professional isolation.

References

American Association for the Advancement of Science. (1967). *Guide for inservice instruction.* Washington, DC: American Association for the Advancement of Science.

American Association for the Advancement of Science. (1989). *Science for all Americans.* New York: Oxford.

Council of State Science Supervisors. (no date). The council of state science supervisors. Retrieved February 18, 2005, from http://csss.enc.org/

Davidson, A. B. (1999). Contracting for safety. *The Science Teacher, 66*(1), 36–39.

Dewey, J. (1902/1990). *The School and Society/The Child and the Curriculum.* Chicago: University of Chicago.

Etheredge, S. & Rudnitsky, A. (2003). *Introducing Students to Scientific Inquiry.* Boston: Allyn and Bacon.

Friedl, A. E. (1986). *Teaching science to children: An integrated approach.* New York: Random House.

GLOBE. (no date). *GLOBE: Learn about GLOBE introduction.* Retrieved March 20, 2003, from http://www.globe.gov/fsl/html/aboutglobe.cgi?intro&lang=en&nav=1

Hart, D. (1994). *Authentic assessment: A handbook for educators.* Menlo Park, CA: Addison-Wesley.

Kahle, J. B., Meece, J. & Scantlebury, K.(2000). Urban African-American middle school science students: Does standards-based teaching make a difference? *Journal of Research in Science Teaching, 37*(9), 1019–1041.

King, K. P. & Thompson, T. E. (1998). Project storm front. *Science Scope, 21*(1), 46.

Marion, R., Hewson, P. W., Tabachnick, B. R., and Blomker, K. B. (1999). Teaching for conceptual change in elementary and secondary science methods courses. *Science Education, 83*(3), 275–307.

National Research Council. (1996). *National Science Education Standards.* National Academy Press: Washington, DC.

Passe, J. (1999). *Elementary School Curriculum.* Boston: McGraw-Hill.

Schneider, R. M., Krajcik, J., & Blumenfeld, P. (in press). Enacting reform-based science materials: The range of teacher enhancements in reform classrooms. *Journal of Research in Science Teaching.*

Sneider, C. I. (1985). *Oobleck: What do scientists do?* Berkeley, CA: Lawrence Hall of Science.

Suping, S. M. (2003). Conceptual change among students in science. Retrieved February 18, 2005, from http://www.ericdigests.org/2004-3/change.html

Supovitz, J. A. & Turner, H. M. (2000). The effects of professional development on science teaching practices and classroom culture. *The Journal of Research in Science Teaching, 37*(9), 963–980.

Wolfinger, D. M. (1984). *Teaching science in the elementary school.* Boston: Little, Brown.

Standards for Assessment in Science Education

CLASSROOM SNAPSHOTS

Spring had arrived at Middleton Middle School, and with the arrival of spring came the annual school science assessment. Mr. Gray, a new teacher in the district, had already been given some hints by more experienced faculty members as to how to get through the experience. It was clear to Mr. Gray that his more senior colleagues considered the assessment experience to be an ordeal and any efficiency that they could add to the process would be welcomed.

The topic used for what was described as the performance-based assessment was plant growth, and the intended outcome was to see how well students could design and implement an experiment that examined variables related to plant growth. It was a good idea in concept. Mr. Gray looked forward to implementing some of his ideas from his student teaching experience, and to involve his students in long-term inquiry with transparent teaching/assessment possibilities was a challenge he anticipated with some relish. As a teacher committed to emphasizing the process skills and habits of mind of a scientist, he was looking forward to assessing students doing science, rather than simply describing it.

Since the available materials were limited—only one set of growing lights for the five sixth-grade teams—the teachers took turns using the materials. Mr. Gray therefore was able to watch the assessment experience carried out three times before he was to receive the materials in the spring. What he observed was most interesting and challenged both his previous experiences and his philosophy of what assessment should look like in the classroom.

The assessment in other classes was done primarily through writing. Students completed activity sheets for the lab investigations they carried out, students composed outlines of the content of each of the chapters of their textbook, students took written quizzes and tests, and students answered questions—in writing—from their textbooks.

While Mr. Gray was not opposed to language and writing experiences, he was concerned about what was actually being assessed. The written materials did a reasonable job of helping teachers judge the quantity of the content knowledge that the students had acquired over the course of the units, but as far as measuring the student's ability to use process skills or evaluate the "habits of mind" (American Association for the Advancement of Science, 1989) associated with the practice of science, they left much to be desired. While the emphasis had so far been on paper and pencil assessment, he was hopeful that more performance-based assessments would become more common as the time drew near for the district's mandated performance-based assessment. Shortly before the first of the sixth-grade teams started the plant study and the related assessment, his mentor gave him a copy of the assessment tool.

Included in the information was a series of steps with which he was quite familiar—they were identical to the colorful "scientific method" poster hanging over the chalkboard in his mentor's room. Not only were the various steps laid out, but students were also given specific quantities of materials to use, the amount of water to be used for both plants, and the two types of fertilizer to be tested. The performance-based assessment of students' ability to carry out their own "fair test"—an experiment—had been reduced in the name of efficiency to a worksheet with a recipe for success. What struck Mr. Gray with blinding clarity was that the only performance that would be assessed would be how well the students followed the directions and filled in the empty spaces in what was essentially a high-stakes worksheet.

There was much that Mr. Gray liked about his colleagues, his students, and his new school, but he questioned the assessment practices. Since he had the luxury of time before the materials were his to use in the spring, Mr. Gray resolved to be true to his philosophy of performance-based assessment. Furthermore he wanted to honor the mentoring he had been receiving and share some of the practices he was going to use with his students with his more senior colleagues.

Changing Emphases

The focus on assessment, as described in the National Science Education Standards, is to measure what is most valued, as opposed to what is most easily assessed. It has always been easier to assess how well students have memorized the names of the bones in the human body or the components of the Krebs Cycle, rather than assessing students on the quality of their thinking and reasoning. While there is, and always will be, a place for mastery of specific content knowledge through memorization, the challenge we face as science teachers is to evaluate the more chimeral, yet more essential, ability of students to think and reason. These changes in how we now conceive science teaching are highlighted in the text of Table 3.1.

Examining and Interpreting the Assessment Standards

New teachers and preservice teachers are well acquainted with assessment, as they have been tested, quizzed, and assessed during their entire academic life. There is, of course, a profound difference between being assessed and developing an assessment to collect meaningful information about what one's students

TABLE 3.1   Changing Emphases for Assessment*

Less Emphasis On	More Emphasis On
Assessing what is easily measured	Assessing what is most highly valued
Assessing discrete knowledge	Assessing rich, well-structured knowledge
Assessing scientific knowledge	Assessing scientific understanding and reasoning
Assessing to learn what students do not know	Assessing to learn what students do understand
Assessing only achievement	Assessing achievement and opportunity to learn
End of term assessments by teachers	Students engaged in ongoing assessment of their work and that of others
Development of external assessments by measurement experts alone	Teachers involved in the development of external assessments

*Reprinted with permission from *National Science Education Standards* © 1996 by the National Academy of Sciences, courtesy of the National Academies Press, Washington, D.C. p. 100.

have learned and then using that information to make a meaningful judgment when interpreting the results of the assessment.

One of the challenges of learning to think about the assessment standards in science is that many new teachers have not had the experience of being assessed in this manner themselves. While most of us can remember experiences involving paper and pencil tests, looking up information in a textbook's glossary, or composing an outline for a chapter in a textbook, the opportunity to be evaluated in the process of *doing* science is generally quite rare.

With the essential theme of the National Science Education Standards being that of promoting inquiry among students as they learn about science, the process of inquiry must be assessed as students are engaging in inquiry—not while they are answering questions about it after the fact. This even relates to some of the basic tasks of learning about science: few teachers will admit to preferring that students have memorized the prefixes for the metric system over the student's ability to measure accurately. Focusing on assessing the knowledge that is most highly valued therefore requires us to watch students carry out developmentally appropriate scientific investigations.

An important element of assessment is the role of formative assessment. "Formative assessment refers to assessments that provide information to students and teachers that is used to improve teaching and learning" (National Research Council, 2001, p. 25). Formative assessment informs the teacher and the student as to how well learning is taking place and emphasizes the need for assessment to be part of the learning process—rather than the customary summative function of assessment at the end of a unit of study.

The National Research Council (NRC) suggests that conducting formative assessment revolves around the teacher asking and answering three questions related to gathering data:

- Where are you trying to go?
- Where are you now?
- How can you get there? (NRC, 2001, p. 26)

While these are very simple questions, the answers the teacher obtains can be profound in terms of making sense of what students know, where the lesson is headed, and what is needed to bridge the difference between what students know now and what you wish them to ultimately learn.

Summative assessment tasks include chapter and unit tests, demonstrations and performances of knowledge gained, creative projects, and final submissions of prepared documents. These assessments are sometimes "high stakes," in a sense, as they are used to make final judgments about what students have learned during a program of study. Historically, these assessments have often been considered a conclusion to learning, though that restrictive view continues to evolve (Beacon Learning Center, no date).

Assessment Standard A

One of the first lessons in developing assessment tools is that they must be aligned with the objectives the teacher wishes to teach in the lesson. Such a process must be designed deliberately. While good information about student learning can be obtained by serendipity and by anecdotal findings, most quality information needs to be obtained thoughtfully and carefully through a deliberately designed assessment tool.

> **ASSESSMENT STANDARD A**
>
> Assessments must be consistent with the decisions they are designed to inform.
>
> - Assessments are deliberately designed.
> - Assessments have explicitly stated purposes.
> - The relationship between the decisions and the data is clear.
> - Assessment procedures are internally consistent.

It is generally accepted that the design of the assessment is guided by the purpose of the assessment and that assessments should have multiple means of collecting information to inform both the teacher and the student (Enger & Yager, 2001). It is also critical to recognize that science is more than simply knowing content knowledge. Enger and Yager (2001) summarize essential components of science—and the areas that we need to concern ourselves with assessing—as the following:

- Concept knowledge: Includes facts, laws, theories, as well as conceptual linkages rather than teaching concepts in isolation. (p. 3)

A **fact** is a "highly corroborated hypothesis that has been so repeatedly tested and for which so much reliable evidence exists, that it would be perverse or irrational to deny it" (Shafersman, 1994). **Laws** represent "generalizations or universal relationships related to the way that some aspect of the natural world behaves under certain conditions" (National Science Teachers Association, 2000, paragraph 7), whereas **theories** are "inferred explanations of some aspect of the natural world. Theories do not become laws even with additional evidence; they explain laws. However, not all scientific laws have accompanying explanatory theories" (National Science Teachers Association, 2000, paragraph 8).

- *Processes:* Includes the classic process skills identified by the American Association for the Advancement of Science during the development of the *Science: A Process Approach* curriculum. These skills—observing, predicting, using space and time relations, classifying, using numbers and quantifying, measuring, communicating, inferring, predicting and controlling variables, interpreting data, formulating hypotheses, defining operationally, and experimenting—form the core experience of *doing* science (Enger & Yager, 2001, p. 4).

- *Applications:* Applying science knowledge asks the students to engage in critical thinking, to apply science knowledge and scientific ways of thinking to real world problems, to evaluate sources of information as well as their quality, and to understand the relationships among science, technology, and society (p. 6).

- *Attitudes:* Examining science-related attitudes involves understanding personal values and the expression of feelings in a constructive manner, the development of more positive attitudes about science, and the development of more effective interpersonal skills (p. 7).

- **Creativity:** Includes assessing students on their ability to demonstrate divergent thinking, to help them consider alternative viewpoints, to generate unusual ideas, to design machines and devices, and to demonstrate multiple means of communicating results (p. 9).

- **Nature of science:** Understanding the nature of science seeks to help students appreciate how to frame questions that can be used to conduct scientific research, to develop and implement methodologies that are used in scientific research, and to learn to cooperate in teams engaged in scientific research (p. 11).

These areas broadly define elements of what constitutes scientific literacy. In terms of developing assessment, the important point to underscore is that the variety of skills and knowledge—content knowledge, affective qualities, problem-solving skills and so on—requires very different assessment strategies and that to ensure that these domains of science education are appropriately assessed requires thoughtful contemplation and evaluation. Watching students engage in science, conducting assessment on a regular basis, and using that assessment to inform instruction are all elements of effective assessment in science teaching.

Related to designing assessment experiences deliberately, assessments must have explicitly stated purposes. Assessment is too great an investment—financially, intellectually, and in terms of the time invested by students—to be used without some specific outcome expected for the teacher, the student, and the larger instructional community. Knowing in advance the intended outcome for the assessment—whether formative or summative—restricts the use of assessment to circumstances that clearly define goals and outcomes associated with the assessment.

The relationship between the decisions and the data is clear when the teacher knows why the assessment is taking place and how the information will be used instructionally. This also includes knowing which type of assessment tool is best suited for gathering the desired type of information. Formal observations using a rubric are excellent for learning how students solve problems and use scientific knowledge. A written test can be appropriate for assessing some measure of content knowledge acquired by students. Knowing the purpose for which the assessment is intended and the type of information desired are the first steps in selecting a meaningful assessment strategy.

SUPPORTING ASSESSMENT STANDARD A: LESSON 3.1

Implementation Idea (Middle School/Secondary): Observational Checklist

This observational checklist provides a tool for teachers to use when assessing students' prior knowledge on a unit on motion. As an introductory activity, students were asked to develop a system that allowed a marble to roll across a table top that would take the greatest amount of time to accomplish this task. The teacher was interested in seeing what sort of informal and prior knowledge about motion the students possessed. The students were divided into six teams, and each group was allowed 20 minutes to create a series of obstacles and adjustments to the table that would increase the amount of time it took for the marble to roll across the table. While the students were working, the teacher paused briefly at each team and both listened actively and interviewed the students about how they were making their decisions regarding the marble's motion.

While making her circuits of the classroom, the teacher used different colored pens to track changes that students made when setting up their apparatus and when responding to her questions.

	Red Team	Orange Team	Yellow Team	Green Team	Blue Team	Purple Team
Momentum						
Energy						
Kinetic Energy						
Potential Energy						
Force						
Friction						
Speed						
Velocity						
Incline						
Time						
Distance						

The assessment tool contained some common terms related to motion. The teacher placed a check mark in the box if she heard students in a group using the term and placed the check mark in parenthesis if the term was being used incorrectly. The blank spaces allowed her to write in comments by students. A completed checklist might appear as the one below:

	Red Team	Orange Team	Yellow Team	Green Team	Blue Team	Purple Team
Momentum		✓	(✓)	(✓)		✓(✓)
Energy		(✓)✓	(✓)✓		✓	
Kinetic Energy		✓			✓	
Potential Energy						
Force	✓	✓	✓			
Friction	✓	✓✓	✓	✓✓	✓	
Speed	✓	✓✓	✓✓	✓✓✓	✓	✓
Velocity	(✓)	(✓)		✓		
Incline	✓		✓	✓		
Time		✓✓✓	✓✓			
Distance		✓✓				✓
"put table on blocks"	✓	✓✓ ✓	✓	✓✓	✓	✓
"make the table bumpy"						✓

✓ = first visit
✓✓ = second visit
✓✓✓ = third visit

In this example, the teacher used the assessment tool to evaluate student knowledge. The term "velocity" was used several times, but not in an appropriate or precise manner. "Momentum" also was used in a more informal sense.

By saving this record, the teacher can carry out the same activity at the end of the unit and obtain a measure of what students learned during the unit and how they were able to apply the knowledge they gained in meeting the marble roll challenge a second time.

SUPPORTING ASSESSMENT STANDARD A: LESSON 3.2

Implementation Idea (Elementary): Mealworm Investigation

The purpose of this investigation is to determine whether mealworms have a preference for dark or light surfaces. Students should be encouraged, based on the materials available, to generate a hypothesis and test the behavior of the mealworms. Among the instructional goals are to help students describe observable behaviors, not to infer emotions or engage in anthropomorphism for the mealworms.

Materials: Mealworms, sheet of paper—1/2 black, 1/2 white, observation sheet, watch or clock.

Investigation: Have the students place the mealworms on the sheet of black/white paper, on the boundary between the two colors. Students should, in advance of the experience, take a position regarding the expected behavior of the mealworms, whether they will move to the light-colored surface, the dark-colored surface, or show no preference. Students may define their investigation in a number of ways, such as setting a time limit, using multiple trials with a single mealworm, or using multiple mealworms to see if, within the boundaries they set for their investigation, the mealworms demonstrate any consistent behaviors. Students would be expected to describe the behavior of the mealworms and cite evidence supporting or rejecting their hypothesis.

Investigation Rubric: Mealworms.

	Accomplished	Developing	Absent
Hypothesis	Students generate a testable question	Students generate a non-testable question	Students begin investigation without creating a meaningful hypothesis
Design (1)	Students design test around hypothesis	Students design a test that is independent of the hypothesis	Students begin investigation without meaningful planning
Design (2)	Students define and control for variables	Students carry out investigation with ill-defined variables	Variables evolve or are not present during investigation
Method	Students consistently follow investigation design they created	Students generally follow investigation design they created	Investigation not related to design students created
Behavior of Mealworms	Behavior of mealworms free from anthropomorphic statements	Mealworm behaviors are anthropomorphic (e.g., "it is afraid," "it likes the color.")	Students make no effort to describe the behavior of the mealworms
Conclusions	Student conclusion (supporting or rejecting hypothesis) supported by data they collected	Conclusions are inconsistent with results and/or hypothesis	Students draw no conclusions

The rubric assumes that students have had some prior independent experiences asking and answering questions in an experimental design setting. Teachers may wish to add another level describing performances that lie between "developing" and "accomplished," depending on the needs of their students.

By using the same assessment rubric during all of the investigations carried out in class, the teacher can track growth among his or her students in terms of how their problem-solving skills develop over the course of the school year. By using the same rubric throughout the district, growth and progress can be meaningfully tracked across large segments of a student's school career.

SUPPORTING ASSESSMENT STANDARD A: LESSON 3.3

Implementation Idea: Using the 5-E Learning Cycle to Embed Assessment into Instruction

This lesson involves some key points drawn from a science unit on simple machines and motion. The information here shows the element of the learning cycle, the activity that corresponds to that element, and some ways that the teacher went about assessing the students' knowledge during a series of lessons.

Learning Cycle Element	Lesson Element	Assessment/Evaluation
Engagement	Teacher shows video clips of rocket launches (this could include *Apollo 13* or *October Sky*, if copyright permission is secured)	KWL: • What do students know about launching rockets? • What is required to launch a rocket? • How does this relate to information we already know about motion?
Exploration	Students create "balloon rockets" and launch rockets on strings across the classroom	Questions from teacher during interviews with students (verbal—recorded as field notes) • What forces are **most** significant at the **beginning** of the balloon's movement? • Why do they decrease across the balloon's path? • What forces are **most** significant near the **end** of the balloon's movement? • Why do they begin to dominate? You will want to examine either distance or velocity as a function of the balloon's circumference. **Sketch** a graph that you believe will predict or best describe the balloon's movement. Graph either the distance or velocity the balloon travels as a function of its circumference.

Explanation	Students present their data	Teacher records student responses and uses them to stress instructional points to ensure accuracy of knowledge gained.
	Teacher responds with clarifying statements and specific connections to content knowledge	Student-led discussion with focus on answers to these questions: • How is the movement of the balloons similar to a rocket? • How is the movement of balloons on a string different from a rocket?
Extension	Students launch model rockets • Students state ahead of time what was learned from the balloon launch and how it will be demonstrated during the rocket launch	Based on student predictions, teacher evaluates them based on: • Accuracy of connections drawn between balloon and rocket launch • Quality of students' explanations linking two different types of launches
Evaluation	Throughout lesson as noted above	

Assessment procedures are internally consistent when all the elements of an assessment process function to give teachers, administrators, and students a coherent and articulated picture of the information derived from the assessment. In the example used in the Classroom Snapshots at the beginning of this chapter, assuming that the results of the plant growth assessment are measures of how students implement their own scientific study is a position that is difficult to defend. Since the example described a practice in which the students are given a very specific set of guidelines to follow, it would be inappropriate to assume that the assessment tools used really assess whether or not students can implement their own study, but rather how well they follow a set of instructions.

Assessment Standard B

ASSESSMENT STANDARD B

Achievement and the opportunity to learn science must be assessed.

■ Achievement data should focus on the science content that is most important for students to learn.
■ Opportunity-to-learn data should focus on the most powerful indicators.
■ Equal attention must be given to the assessment of the opportunity to learn and to the assessment of student achievement.

The fundamental experience of science in the public schools is to engage in learning through a process of inquiry. As stated in the National Science Education Standards:

Inquiry is central to science learning. When engaging in inquiry, students describe objects and events, ask questions, construct explanations, test those explanations against current scientific knowledge, and communicate their ideas to others. They identify their assumptions, use critical and logical thinking, and consider alternative explanations. In this

SUPPORTING ASSESSMENT STANDARD B: LESSON 3.4

Aligning Assessment Practice with Knowledge and Skills to Be Assessed

The following chart may assist in the identification of assessment practices and the knowledge or skills that you wish to assess. The concept or skill to be assessed is on the vertical axis; an assessment strategy is noted along the horizontal axis. The shaded area notes a potential intersection between a means of assessment and an item to be assessed.

	Structured observation	Student self-report	Clinical interviewing	Journaling	Concept map construction	Open-ended questioning	Structured questions	Written examinations	Product construction
Observing	▓	▓	▓	▓			▓		
Communicating	▓	▓	▓	▓			▓		
Measuring	▓	▓	▓	▓			▓		
Classifying	▓	▓	▓	▓			▓		
Predicting	▓	▓	▓	▓	▓	▓	▓		
Inferring	▓	▓	▓	▓	▓	▓	▓		
Controlling variables	▓	▓	▓	▓					▓
Defining operationally	▓	▓	▓	▓					▓
Interpreting data	▓	▓	▓	▓	▓	▓	▓		
Experimenting	▓	▓	▓	▓					▓
Formulating models	▓	▓	▓	▓	▓				▓
Demonstration of content knowledge	▓	▓	▓	▓			▓	▓	▓

What appears from the chart above is that assessing science skills can be accomplished more effectively when there is a relationship between what the student is doing and what the teacher is looking for. Generally, this is not present in objective testing. Structured questions and written examinations will always have a place in the classroom, but it is important to consider what is being learned and how best to assess the knowledge or skills. The more sophisticated process skills—often referred to as "integrated process skills"—are better assessed when there is an opportunity for teachers to probe more deeply for student understanding than is possible on a structured examination.

way, students actively develop their understanding of science by combining scientific knowledge with reasoning and thinking skills. (1996, p. 2)

The consequence of this statement, as it relates to assessment, is that achievement data should focus on the science content that is most important for students to learn. What is judged to be most important to learn goes beyond the simple (and sometimes complicated) facts of content knowledge, but includes how students perform science, how students think in scientific ways, and how students use their powers of reasoning to obtain defensible answers to the questions they pose. In a relative sense, it is a fairly straightforward task to measure static knowledge—facts and figures—"inert knowledge," as stated wryly in the NSES. The need to assess the active parts of science—the process of inquiry, the ability to communicate findings, and the ability to use science knowledge and scientific ways of thinking to make personal decisions and prepare for personal social action—is more difficult to assess by traditional paper and pencil methods.

Opportunity-to-learn data should focus on the most powerful indicators, such as teacher content and pedagogical knowledge, understanding of students, and the nature of the school's curriculum. These opportunity-to-learn factors profoundly affect the nature and quality of the students' learning experiences. In a very real sense, the student's ability to learn science is based on the teacher's ability to teach science.

SUPPORTING ASSESSMENT STANDARD B: LESSON 3.5

Assessment Idea: Opportunity to Learn

The notion of "opportunity to learn" is part of an effort to ensure equity and fairness for all students. Bond, Moss, and Carr (1996) note the importance of ensuring students' opportunity to learn:

1. When assessments are used for high stakes decisions, such as promotion for graduation, it is a legal and ethical responsibility to ensure that students have had the opportunity to acquire the capabilities for which they are held accountable.
2. It is essential to know about curricular validity both to understand test results and to enable reform of policy and practice.
3. It must be recognized that assessments not only document the success of past learning opportunities, but also constrain or enable future learning opportunities.
4. Legal precedents are implicated if student assessments have an adverse impact on students because of their race, national origin, gender, or disability. (paragraph 4)

The opportunity to learn, then, asks that teachers, administrators, and science education systems assess students fairly, that they ensure that assessment practices reflect what children have been exposed to during their time in science classes, and that the assessment instruments do not demonstrate bias against any or all students.

At the classroom level, the teacher's knowledge and training is an important element in students' opportunities to learn. Work by King, Shumow, and Lietz (2001) notes the potential for wholesale disenfranchisement of students in situations where teacher preparation is minimal. Other issues to be aware of—and be vigilant of—include the availability of materials for students to use in class, time allotted to science instruction, as well as large-scale demographic data, such as per-student funding in the school district and the socioeconomic status of the local community. Many of these issues are structural issues beyond the control of individual classroom teachers, but awareness and a commitment to helping all students learn—and be fairly assessed—*is* the responsibility of a classroom teacher.

Equal attention must be given to the assessment of an opportunity to learn and to the assessment of student achievement. In the politically charged area of standardized testing, opportunity to learn takes on an even more critical meaning. Students who are assessed and being held accountable for science knowledge by the state have a right to be exposed to science concepts and experiences taught in a meaningful and engaging manner. Assessment is both formative and summative. Formative assessment, as described above, helps teachers make instructional decisions and, when used effectively, becomes a transparent part of the teaching and learning process. Assessment is *measuring* student learning through a variety of strategies. *Evaluation* involves making a judgment as to what the data collected during the assessment process means. The process of evaluation should extend equally to the student and to the teacher, helping the teacher to judge his or her teaching practices and how students are learning; for the students, the process allows them to make judgments about how well they are learning and what areas need additional attention.

Assessment Standard C

A fundamental tenant of assessment is the notion of validity. For an assessment practice to be valid, it must actually measure the feature that it claims to measure. Looking back to the vignette that opened this chapter, one of Mr. Gray's fundamental concerns about his school's assessment practice was that it did not measure what it claimed to measure. Student inquiry was not the real outcome of the experience; following directions to complete a science activity was the emphasis. As another example, asking students to measure objects with a meter stick or with a set of calipers can be used to demonstrate mastery of that particular measurement skill. Asking students to name the parts of a set of calipers does not really measure how effectively students can measure. The goal is to ensure that the feature that is claimed to be measured is *actually measured.*

ASSESSMENT STANDARD C

The technical quality of the data collected is well matched to the decisions and actions taken on the basis of their interpretation.

- The feature that is claimed to be measured is actually measured.
- Assessment tasks are authentic.
- An individual student's performance is similar on two or more tasks that claim to measure the same aspect of student achievement.
- Students have adequate opportunity to demonstrate their achievements.
- Assessment tasks and methods of presenting them provide data that are sufficiently stable to lead to the same decisions if used at different times.

SUPPORTING ASSESSMENT STANDARD C: LESSON 3.6

Implementation Idea: Authentic Assessment

A commonly used investigation for students in the upper elementary and middle school grades is testing various brands of paper towels for either strength or absorbency. A variety of powerful skills are embedded into this experience:

- Problem solving
- Testing hypotheses
- Data collection and analysis
- Defending a proposition
- Developing operational definitions

Suppose a classroom, divided into six student teams, is asked to rank five samples of paper towels from 1 through 5 (from most absorbent to least absorbent) and generates the following results:

Team Brand	Red Team	Orange Team	Yellow Team	Green Team	Blue Team	Purple Team
A	3	3	3	3	3	3
B	4	4	4	4	4	4
C	1	2	1	1	1	2
D	2	1	2	2	2	1
E	5	5	5	5	5	5

What is interesting about the results obtained by the students and organized in the table above is that there is a difference of opinion regarding which brand of paper towel—Brand C or Brand D—is actually the most absorbent. The opportunity for students to debate and discuss these results opens up the discipline of science as a learning experience that is open to argument and explanation. As a teacher, you will want to encourage this; similarly, you will want to look for evidence of problem solving from among your students as they work out *why* there are seemingly two "right" answers to their investigation.

A scoring rubric for this sort of discussion among student teams might look like this:

Class Discussion of Results (4 points)

_____ 4   Students demonstrate all of the following in an exemplary manner: (1) students provide operational definitions of relevant variables; (2) students provide operational definitions of procedures used during investigation; (3) students challenge (diplomatically) other interpretations of results or accept (gracefully) challenges to their interpretation.

_____ 3   Students demonstrate all of the following: (1) students provide operational definitions of relevant variables; (2) students provide operational definitions of procedures used during investigation; (3) students challenge (diplomatically) other interpretations of results or accept (gracefully) challenges to their interpretation.

_____ 2   Students demonstrate two of the following: (1) students provide operational definitions of relevant variables; (2) students provide operational definitions of procedures used during investigation; (3) students challenge (diplomatically) other interpretations of results or accept (gracefully) challenges to their interpretation.

_____ 1   Students demonstrate one of the following: (1) students provide operational definitions of relevant variables; (2) students provide operational definitions of procedures used during investigation; (3) students challenge (diplomatically) other interpretations of results or accept (gracefully) challenges to their interpretation.

_____ 0   Students do not demonstrate any of the above behaviors.

Rubrics such as this can be challenging to develop, but they are valuable tools in looking for *behaviors* in students that are more difficult to assess through traditional paper and pencil means. For the teacher, rubrics also require practice to become proficient in their use, especially when compared with objectively written tests.

Assistance in preparing rubrics has been made more efficient through technological tools such as Rubistar (http://rubistar.4teachers.org/index.php). The interface at Rubistar helps teachers to conceive and construct useful rubrics for classroom assessment. Another helpful Web site is Rubric Builder (http://landmark-project.com/classweb/tools/rubric_builder.php3). Visit both sites to get a "feel" for the interface and determine which one works best for you as you develop assessment tools.

Assessment tasks are authentic. In this sense, the assessment strategy that is being used resembles the skill that is being measured. Assessing a skill such as classification demonstrates a higher level of authenticity when it involves observing students classify objects or information, rather than having students describe various types of classification models.

A companion to the concept of validity is the notion of reliability in assessment practices. Reliability requires that an individual student's performance is similar on two or more tasks that claim to measure the same aspect of student achievement. As an example, if a student can develop a hypothesis for future investigation in both the life sciences and the physical sciences (assuming the student has had an opportunity to learn both subject areas), then an assessment tool that records the student's ability to create hypotheses may be deemed to be reliable. In essence, the same skill is being measured from multiple perspectives, and the results obtained by the assessment tool are consistent.

Students must have adequate opportunities to demonstrate their achievements. The opportunity to demonstrate their competency must also be fair, developmentally appropriate, and the assessment and the experience being assessed must be similar, for example, performance assessments to measure student performances of science. In addition to issues of developmental appropriateness for the skills being assessed, it is also critical that the written parts of any test be appropriate to the student's reading ability, so that the assessment remains anchored in assessing science, rather than creating a barrier to learning and assessment caused by the student's inability to read the material.

From a teacher's perspective, it is helpful to assess the same skill using multiple assessments in an effort to "triangulate" the information to be sure that the teacher is accurately measuring what the student is expected to be learning. To build upon the opening vignette, Mr. Gray was interested in assessing how students were able to test hypotheses by devising a fair test of a student-generated question. In addition to having students perform a test and capturing observations of students engaged in inquiry, he could also assess in a paper and pencil manner students' understanding of what made one test of a hypothesis fair and what made another one biased. He could also interview students to see how they developed and implemented their study. Another option may be to have his students present their findings during a "scientific convention," where students could explain not only the questions they were testing, but explain the reasoning behind developing their questions, developing their methodology, and how they used the data they collected to support their conclusions.

Another element of reliability, as stated in the NSES, is related to large-scale assessments of large groups of students. For these large assessments to have meaning, the tasks and the methods must yield stable results; that is, they must generate data that does not change unduly over time or between groups. This allows for appropriate inferences to be drawn as student progress is measured over time. As stated previously, the task/experience being measured and the assessment given must be consistent.

Given also that these sorts of assessments are used by policy makers, parents, and community members to assess the quality of school experiences, the technical quality of the assessment is related to public confidence in the assessment. "This public confidence is influenced by the extent to which technical quality has been considered by educators and policy makers and the skill with which they communicated with the public about it" (National Research Council, 1996, p. 85).

Assessment Standard D

A premise of the National Science Education Standards is that all students should have access to quality science education and should be expected to achieve scientific literacy" (National Research Council, 1996, p. 85). This notion of science for all children is also emphasized in the American Association for the Advancement of Science's (AAAS) *Science for all Americans*. Both the AAAS and the National Academy of Sciences recognize that science is a pursuit that is important for all, and to ensure that "science for all Americans" becomes a reality, the ways that we measure how students learn science must likewise meet the needs of all young people.

The fundamental issue in Assessment Standard D is that the assessment practices must be fair to all students. As assessments are developed, both for large-scale and individual classroom use, it is critical that the assessment tools measure what students know about science, rather than providing evidence about where the students grew up, how much money their family has, or what ethnicity or race they claim. Assessments must be vigilant so they do not perpetuate stereotypes or assume that all students share certain sets of life experiences. In addition, concerns about language—both in communicating the intention of the assessment and avoiding language constructions that might be offensive to some groups—should be addressed while developing assessment tools.

> **ASSESSMENT STANDARD D**
>
> Assessment practices must be fair.
>
> - Assessment tasks must be reviewed for the use of stereotypes, for assumptions that reflect the perspectives or experiences of a particular group, for language that might be offensive to a particular group, and for other features that might distract students from the intended task.
> - Large-scale assessments must use statistical techniques to identify potential bias among subgroups.
> - Assessment tasks must be appropriately modified to accommodate the needs of students with physical disabilities, learning disabilities, or limited English proficiency.
> - Assessment tasks must be set in a variety of contexts, be engaging to students with different interests and experiences, and must not assume the perspective or experience of a particular gender, racial, or ethnic group.

As high-stakes assessments have become more and more a part of life in education, it can be helpful—to ensure that student knowledge is accurately assessed—to use assessments structured similarly to the tests students will be taking. This is not to suggest that performance-based assessment doesn't have a place in the science classroom, but as the multiple-choice/reading-intensive tests become an annual part of the life of students, including similar assessment models in your own teaching—as part of a broad set of assessment tools—can be of value to students in assuring that what they know is really being assessed. As you will likely encounter administrators and department chairs who will insist on this, being ready for this sort of assessment before becoming a teacher is preferable to being taken aback once one has entered the profession.

SUPPORTING ASSESSMENT STANDARD D: LESSON 3.7

Implementation Idea: Developing Assessments Similar to State/District Assessments

This is a series of sample questions taken from an in-class assessment given by a secondary science teacher. The main departure from classic high-stakes assessments that this teacher made is that there are opportunities for students to make open responses to the questions, as opposed to forced choices.

A student collected data during an investigation of the properties of centripetal force. Using the data table below, answer the questions that follow.

DATA

Mass (in rubber stoppers)	Force (washers)	Radius (m)	Time (30 revolutions)
1	30	1.0	36.5
2	30	1.0	51.6
3	30	1.0	63.2
4	30	1.0	73.0
5	30	1.0	81.6

CALCULATIONS

Distance (m)	Time (s)	Velocity (m/s)

Note: $C = 2\pi R$, $v = d/t$

In this investigation, you varied the mass of the rubber stoppers following the circular path in each trial. Therefore, the radius is the independent variable. Plot a graph that best demonstrates the relationship between the variables you tested. What does the shape of the plot reveal about the relationship between the two variables?

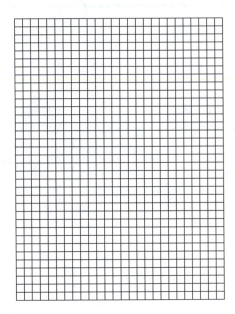

Compose a summary statement regarding the relationships you discovered among force, speed, and centripetal force. Use the numerical data you derived in your investigation to support the conclusions you reach. Using the equation for centripetal force, explain how the results of your investigation are consistent or inconsistent with this equation. Include a response to that question in your summary.

In addition, include answers to the following in your response:

■ What variables were kept constant
■ Which variables were allowed to change
■ Whether or not the prediction was supported by the evidence
■ The meaning behind the relationship demonstrated by the variables
■ How the data is consistent or inconsistent with the relation

$$F_{centripetal} = 4\pi^2 R/T^2$$

Large-scale assessments must use statistical techniques to identify potential bias among subgroups. This relates to the investment of resources that must be employed while developing assessment tools, especially on a large scale. For classroom teachers, while your involvement in the development of large-scale instruments is unlikely, it is important to be thoughtful in the construction of your tests and other assessment tools. What ends up with statistics being used to demonstrate the appropriateness of an assessment tool often starts with a thoughtful consideration of where the student comes from and the sort of life they live. Again, from the perspective of the classroom teacher, if the large-scale tests are reliable, valid, and do not unduly discriminate among the various constituencies of students that will take the assessment, helpful—and often alarming—information can be derived from how students of different racial, ethnic, social, and economic backgrounds are succeeding in the science classroom. This can provide some hard evidence for the teacher to use when developing better ways to meet the needs of these children.

"Science for all Americans" must also include assessment tasks and practices that fairly assess students of limited English proficiency, students with physical impairments, and students with learning disabilities. The purpose of the assessment is to gather data about what the student knows about science, rather than what his or her barriers to learning science might be.

Assessment tasks must be set in a variety of contexts, be engaging to students with different interests and experiences, and must not assume the perspective or experience of a particular gender, racial, or ethnic group" (National Research Council, 1996, p. 86). In my experience as a high school science teacher, I once had a colleague who used examples from his own life growing up on a farm ("How tall is a silo?" started one brainstorming activity). This was certainly an appropriate example to be used with his peers from the small, rural community where he grew up, but in the large suburban school where he taught, it was an example of how one person's experiences were completely alien to the experiences of others. While using the silo example as a departure point for brainstorming was not technically "unfair," it did underscore to my colleague the need to have students and teachers share a common perspective and to ensure that the assessment practices matched what the students were taught—and all within a meaningful context. More egregious examples might be to use language unfamiliar to students on a written examination or to assess students on information that they have not been exposed to. While one should be incredulous that this can happen, many readers may remember taking a well-used examination, only to realize partway through the exam that while it may have been a good assessment for the instructor's course three years previously, it did not reflect the material taught during *that* semester.

The point, then, is that teachers must be vigilant in assuring that all students can make use of the assessments that they create. Bias—whether intentional or not—should not provide an additional barrier to learning or to assessment practices.

Assessment Standard E

As with planning lessons, there must be an alignment between the objectives created for a lesson and the means by which the lesson is assessed. The meaning that the teacher attaches to the assessment and to the outcome it offers must be defensible and supported by the relationship between what was taught and what was assessed.

Objectives help teachers plan their instructional goals. Specific objectives for a lesson are derived from broad instructional goals defined for a unit of study; they may also be seen as being derived from state and local learning standards.

ASSESSMENT STANDARD E

The inferences made from assessments about student achievement and opportunity to learn must be sound.

■ When making inferences from assessment data about student achievement and opportunity to learn science, explicit reference needs to be made to the assumptions on which the inferences are based.

What makes learning objectives useful for the teacher may include the following:

■ The objective is aligned with the unit of study.

■ The objective can be meaningfully aligned with an assessment practice.

■ The objective and the assessment are developed in tandem with each other.

■ The objective identifies the level of proficiency expected by the teacher to indicate that the student has met the standard.

These implications can be subject to various interpretations: if a teacher-created assessment results in a large number of students receiving low scores on the assessment, this could be a function of any or all of the following:

■ The assessment was "too hard" or was not designed with appropriate developmental considerations in mind.

■ The students were not prepared for the assessment.

■ The assessment and the teaching/learning experiences were inconsistent with each other.

■ There were cultural or language biases that prevented the students from demonstrating their knowledge.

SUPPORTING ASSESSMENT STANDARD E: LESSON 3.8

Aligning Objectives and Assessments

While no list of this sort can ever claim to be comprehensive, it does offer a few examples of learning objectives and approaches for assessing the objectives as they are written. Keep in mind also that because these learning objectives are presented here, out of context for a broader science unit, any issues related to how the objectives are drawn from broader unit goals cannot be addressed.

Objective: *Students will generate a testable hypothesis using an "if _____ then _____" structure.*

Possible assessments: Note that the teacher will need to identify two separate but related issues:

1. The teacher will examine student-written materials to see if a hypothesis is composed in a manner consistent with the "if-then" model;
2. The teacher will need to make a judgment as to whether the hypothesis is "testable."

The objective above is measurable—as defined by the assessment statements—and seeks to offer a sense of how students perform scientific inquiry.

Objective: *Students will demonstrate their understanding of force and motion concepts by applying their knowledge to the challenge of moving a rolling marble through a series of obstacles.*

Assessment: As in the example cited previously (Lesson 3.1), a teacher can observe how students are arranging obstacles on the inclined plane. Asking questions of the students, such as "what effect does adding the extra meter sticks to the table top have?" will help the teacher assess how the students are applying their knowledge of force and motion to solve a specific problem.

As an additional resource, the *Science Educator's Guide to Laboratory Assessment* (Doran, Chan, Tamir & Lenhardt, 2002) offers additional assistance in creating meaningful assessments in the laboratory setting across all the science disciplines.

This underscores the challenges associated with not only creating and administering tests, but the potential challenges associated with interpreting them. These issues become more and more critical as elements of the No Child Left Behind Act become a part of every teacher's practice, as low outcomes on high-stakes standardized tests will have grave consequences for schools, teachers, administrators, and, at the heart of the experience, the children who will be taking these tests.

Implications for Practice

The challenges of assessment are varied. At the very least, ethics suggest that all students should be assessed fairly, that assessment practices be consistent with what is being taught, and that assessment practices lead to continued learning. The classroom teacher has to juggle multiple elements of assessment itself: classroom behavior, the student's level of effort, and the student's classroom behavior; short-term and long-term assessments; individual and group assessments; and content knowledge and process skills (Anderson, 2003).

More broadly, Chatterji (2003) related the elements of the U.S. Department of Labor's instructional goals for high school graduates, stating that by the end of high school, students should be able to engage in the following behaviors:

- decision making
- problem solving
- communication
- mathematical applications
- learning how to learn
- cooperative teamwork
- leadership
- self-management (p. 16)

Chatterji used these to underscore the point that assessment increasingly relates to more abstract, process-oriented skills in addition to the traditional content goals often associated with testing and assessment. It is also abundantly clear that movement across the disciplines is more toward process-oriented and problem-solving skills. Science, a rich discipline with both abundant content knowledge and a considerable understanding of the process skills, is an area that is naturally assessed by performance-based assessments.

The commitment to performance-based assessment also requires careful reflection and preparation by teachers who will be using these tools. This short list—by no means exhaustive—outlines the many issues that must be considered as educational systems move toward the inclusion of more performance-based experiences for students:

- The current knowledge of classroom teachers with respect to performance-based assessment
- The vision of what assessment should look like in the future and how educational institutions can arrive there
- The increasing role that assessment will take in the schools
- Assessment as a means to improve instruction versus assessment as an end in itself
- Accommodating students with disabilities
- Accommodating students whose native language is not English

- Assessment as an element of educational reform
- How data from assessments will be used—both on a classroom level and on a systemic level
- How policy makers will use the assessment data that emerges (Lissitz & Schafer, 2002, pp. v-vi)

The less tangible nature of the process skills and problem-solving elements of learning and assessing science makes the imperative for multiple means of assessment greater still (Ardovino, Hollingsworth & Ybarra, 2000). The burden of triangulating assessment from multiple perspectives, combined with the greater call for assessment from policy makers, places the teacher in an unenviable situation. Among the options available, the most reasonable approach is to find ways for the boundaries between assessment and teaching to become more transparent—moving toward a teaching and learning model in which multiple assessment practices become part of the teaching process. Instructional models, such as the 5-E Learning Cycle (c.f., Carin & Bass, 2001), might offer teachers an instructional approach that also assists them as they attend to their professional obligation to assess students more frequently.

An additional challenge of assessment is the movement of resources to support testing practices. In trying economic times, the additional costs of standardized assessments (ranging from $0.54 to over $10 per student, in 1996 dollars) places additional burdens upon already over-taxed school systems (Hardy, 1996). Given that some elementary schools support science teaching at a level of $0.50 per child—per *year*—it is clear that testing must be made efficient, meaningful, and become as much of the teaching and learning process as possible.

CLASSROOM SNAPSHOTS

NSES-Informed Assessment Practices

Two years later, the assessment practices in his school were undergoing an evolution. Mr. Gray recognized several things at the outset. The most important was that his colleagues were not going to change their practices overnight and that he would have to demonstrate some success with performance-based assessment practices before his colleagues would "buy in" to the practices he advocated. As his first ally, he enlisted his department chair, Ms. Violet.

During a pre-observation discussion before one of the five observations that nontenured teachers in his building received, he shared with her his interest in moving his assessment into a more performance-based direction. She was open to the idea and promised to offer him feedback on how she perceived his success engaging his students in performance-based assessments.

The assessment went very well. Mr. Gray had created a performance assessment rubric that took on what he knew would be the objections of a number of his colleagues. First, the rubric was manageable. It focused on specific skills related to the performances he judged to be of most worth and allowed for efficient note taking and recording of student performances. Each of the elements on his rubric had four levels of performance, which were carefully defined and established discrete levels of performance (Hammerman & Musial, 1994). Mr. Gray was able to collect his information efficiently and organize it in such a way to draw some conclusions regarding his teaching and his students' learning.

The feedback from Ms. Violet was also helpful, both in terms of his teaching and assessment practices, but also in that it encouraged her to share some of his practices at the next faculty meeting.

The next faculty meeting did not start with announcements, but with Mr. Gray's challenge: If physical education teachers can do performance-based assessment, why can't science teachers? To introduce the idea, he asked the teachers to compare a variety of popcorn samples purchased at a local supermarket, basing his idea on one he read in a science teaching journal (Rosenzweig, 1996). While they compared quality, price, and "popabililty," Mr. Gray collected data on a behavioral checklist and shared his findings with them at the conclusion of their investigations. With the addition of butter and salt for the popcorn, the activity offered a good foundation for the faculty to discuss their assessment practices—and what it means to be able to do science. Among the intriguing discoveries was that each group of teachers examined a different property of the popcorn, but Mr. Gray's feedback suggested that they all created their own fair test of the questions they posed. Why, then, couldn't students do the same thing with the annual plant investigation—and more?

That meeting started a new emphasis on assessment at Middleton Middle School. Movement toward assessing performance in science was slow, but continual. To the principal's gratification, test scores did not decrease. In fact, the teachers found that engaging students in inquiry practices raised the overall level of discourse in the classroom and helped the students become better problem solvers. Teachers themselves were more engaged in the process of assessment; with performance assessment, it was more like teaching than grading. Discussions with students involved more conversations about how to solve problems and use their existing knowledge as well as how to defend the answers they obtained. The future looks promising for the teachers and students of Middleton Middle School.

Mr. Gray, for his part, found his role as a teacher-leader to be not only professionally rewarding, but personally rewarding as well. The challenge of sharing the practices he valued with his colleagues—and having them embrace them as well—was consistent with his personal vision of teachers as lifelong learners.

The practices described in the opening and closing vignettes—starting with an assessment of how students carried out a specific investigation to assessing how students solve problems—is not a great stretch for teachers. Often what is needed is simply a new perspective on what is being done and asking objectively if this experience is really what we want to measure. Clearly, following guidelines to show how a problem can be solved is an important first step in helping students to ask and answer their own questions. But ensuring that the teacher and the school community use these procedural skills as a beginning point for deeper understanding is the long-term goal and is more consistent with the National Science Education Standards' goals of lifelong learning and problem solving.

Summary

- More effective assessment of student learning requires moving from what is most easily assessed toward assessing the knowledge and thinking skills that are most important.

- Assessing discrete knowledge and scientific knowledge is part of the assessment process. With a movement toward performance-based and authentic assessment practices, teachers are taking on the challenge of determining not only what students know, but how they solve problems and use information in novel settings. A commitment to authentic assessment ensures that what we assess resembles as much as possible the knowledge we want students to demonstrate.

- More than simply using assessment to demonstrate what students don't know—or measuring only content knowledge achievement—assessment practices in science are working to better capture data on how students learn and solve problems, as well as how they develop their own opportunities for further constructing their own knowledge.

- Assessment practices are becoming a more seamless part of the learning process. Rather than assessing mostly accumulated knowledge at the end of a unit of study, more and more we find assessment taking place continuously throughout the instructional program, ensuring that teachers capture what students know at each point along a unit of study.

- Teachers have the opportunity to develop their own assessment within school districts and schools, rather than relying exclusively on external assessments. Ensuring that district and school-specific assessments are in place gives teachers data about what students are learning and how to improve instruction throughout an entire science education system.

References

American Association for the Advancement of Science. (1989). *Science for all Americans.* New York: Oxford.

Anderson, L. W. (2003). *Classroom assessment.* Mahwah, NJ: Lawrence Erlbaum Associates.

Ardovino, J., Hollingsworth, J. & Ybarra, S. (2000). *Multiple measures.* Thousand Oaks, CA: Corwin.

Beacon Learning Center. (no date). *Assessment-inquiry connection.* Retrieved March 10, 2005, from http://www.justsciencenow.com/assessment/

Bond, L., Moss, P., & Carr, P. (1996, April). Fairness in large-scale performance assessment. In G. W. Phillips (Ed.), Technical issues in large scale performance assessment (pp. 117–140). Washington, D.C.: National Center for Education Statistics, U.S. Department of Education.

Carin, A. A. & Bass, J. E. (2001). *Methods of teaching science as inquiry.* Upper Saddle River, NJ: Merrill/Prentice Hall.

Chatterji, M. (2003). *Designing and using tools for educational assessment.* Boston: Allyn & Bacon.

Doran, R, Chan, F., Tamir, P. & Lenhardt, C. (2002). *Science educator's guide to laboratory assessment.* Arlington, VA: National Science Teachers Association.

Enger, S. K. & Yager, R. E. (2001). *Assessing student understanding in science.* Thousand Oaks, CA: Corwin.

Hammerman, E. & Musial, D. (1994). *Performances of most worth.* Glen Ellyn, IL: Institute for Educational Research.

Hardy, R. (1997). Examining the costs of performance assessment. In Kane, M. B. & Mitchell, R. (Eds.) *Implementing performance assessment:* Promises, Problems, and Challenges. Hillsdale, NJ: Lawrence Erlbaum Associates.

King, K. P., Shumow, L., & Lietz, S. (2001). Science education in an urban elementary school: Case studies of teacher beliefs and classroom practices. *Science Education, 85*(2), 89–110.

Lissitz, R. W. & Schafer, W. D. (2002). *Assessment in educational reform.* Boston: Allyn & Bacon.

National Research Council. (1996). *National Science Education Standards.* National Academy Press: Washington, DC.

National Research Council. (2001). *Classroom assessment and the National Science Education Standards.* Washington, DC: National Academy Press.

National Science Teachers Association. (2000). *NSTA position statement: The nature of science.* Retrieved March 10, 2005, from http://www.nsta.org/positionstatement&psid=22&print=y

North Central Regional Educational Laboratory. (no date). *Opportunity to learn.* Retrieved March 11, 2005, from http://edstar.ncrel.org/mn/ViewEssay.asp?IssueID=37&EssayID=151

Rosenzweig, B. (1996). Popcorn possibilities. *Science Scope, 19*(4), 22.

Shafersman, S. D. (1994). *Scientific thinking and the scientific method.* Retrieved March 10, 2005, from http://www.freeinquiry.com/intro-to-sci.html

CHAPTER 4

Standards for Science Content

CLASSROOM SNAPSHOTS

Carl had loved science for as long as he could remember. As a student, he had good-naturedly pestered his teachers with questions that always started with "how" and "why?" By eight, he had his own chemistry set and was keeping his own lab notebook describing his investigations. The "Question" page at the back of the book had slowly moved forward, as he had dozens of questions that his investigations had provoked. Needless to say, when he entered high school, he was excited about the prospects of learning more about science from real experts in the field.

The first day of class encouraged his excitement: the teacher, Mr. Beebe, shared with his students his interest in the field of biology, his expectations for hard work, and his expectations for excellence. When assigned his weighty biology text for the school year, Carl could almost feel the knowledge bound up in the book trying to leak out and help him answer his questions.

The next day, Carl was ready to go. He'd tucked his old lab notebook into his book bag, and the night before he had marked some of the biology-related questions that he had recorded previously. Taking his seat at the lab table, he looked around the classroom and wondered which of the apparatus stored behind the glass-walled cabinets they would be using first. Mr. Beebe encouraged Carl's interest by opening class with the remark that they were not going to waste any time—there was much to learn, and the work would start today. Reaching into a manila folder on his demonstration table, Mr. Beebe then passed out a thick sheaf of papers to each student. "An experiment," Carl said to himself, wondering where they would begin.

As the papers were finding their way around the room, Mr. Beebe said, "The best resource for completing these questions is your biology textbook. You might start with the glossary to help define the terms on the worksheet. I'll be collecting these on Friday, so you have four class periods to complete them. Good luck and I'll be here to help you if you're having trouble finding the information."

The worksheet—all six pages of it—arrived in Carl's hands. The directions were simple: define the terms listed below. There were over fifty terms. Many of the words were familiar from previous science classes: observation, inference, variables . . . while some were more specific to the biology class: osmosis, diffusion, membrane. Eager to do a good job, Carl prepared to start, while glancing once more at the lab tools on the shelves, defining the terms on the worksheet, using the textbook as his source of information.

Carl returned to class the next day with the entire worksheet completed. Mr. Beebe looked stunned, and then smiled and said, "You're quite a scientist, aren't you? This assignment was supposed to take all week—so you can do something else during class for the next couple of days. Either that or you can help your lab partner find some of the answers. Just hold on to this for me, will you? We'll go over the answers in class on Friday."

Carl was stunned! Science class had become a study hall instead of a place to get his questions answered. Reluctantly, Carl went back to his lab table, exchanged a few words with his lab partner, and then pulled out a novel for his literature class. He glanced up at the lab equipment and sensed that it would be a while before he was going to get to use any of it.

Introduction

Not all students who enter the science classroom on the first day are as ambitious or as enthusiastic as Carl. Nor are worksheets a "bad" thing. But the practice of learning science exclusively through reading a textbook and recording answers on worksheets is generally inconsistent with the vision of teaching science through inquiry.

Many students enter the science classroom either neutral or ambivalent—and even at times with an active dislike. The scenario profiled above is less common than it once was, but it is still present in far too many places. Students in a class such as Mr. Beebe's might have their interest in science extinguished completely; those who have little or no interest to start with will remain at best neutral—or at worst antagonistic—toward the whole notion of learning science.

The themes presented in *Horace's Compromise* (Sizer, 1992) are abundantly clear in Mr. Beebe's instructional methodology. In Sizer's book, the composite character Horace Smith, an admirable person and teacher, wants the best for his students, but he reaches a "compromise" with them—and, more importantly, with himself—by creating an academic dance among beliefs, achievable goals, and the grind of daily teaching that ultimately produces docile students and docile teachers that shepherd them. Charles Silberman wrote of this during his exhaustive study of schools in the 1960s (Silberman, 1970). The academic result—requiring only modest intellectual engagement from students in exchange for docile behavior, making the management of classes a simpler matter—has been well documented in the literature. Mr. Beebe's classroom strategies, profiled above, asks the student to learn a modest amount of science content and the teacher to invest a modest amount of easily managed effort.

Also well documented by science education scholars are findings such as those by Shymansky (Shymansky, 1989; Shymansky, 1990; Shymanksy, Hedges & Woodword, 1990), which provide ample evidence that inquiry-based experiences in science typically teach as much content as do textbook-driven curricula, but that students also demonstrate greater curiosity, greater problem-solving skills, and a better ability to understand and apply science process skills. The foundation that inquiry-rich elementary experiences provides for students should be further developed in the middle and high school classroom and is most appropriately developed when the central focus of the secondary experience is student-driven inquiry.

Changing Emphases

The changes outlined in the content standards are not about *changing* the content to be mastered by students as they move through the K–12 educational system, but about how the content knowledge is obtained and how it relates to a larger body of content knowledge. Broadly conceived, the changes proposed for the content standards move away from learning facts in isolation toward learning about factual scientific information in context. The approach to learning science content focuses more on processes of scientific inquiry than memorization, as well as integrating all aspects of science content and processes into a seamless advance of inquiry and content development. A primary goal of the content standards is to move away from learning vast amounts of science content superficially and into studying a few fundamental science concepts in greater depth. This evolution in practice is summarized in Table 4.1.

As you read and discuss this chapter, please note how the science content identified for inclusion is defined more broadly than perhaps you are accustomed to covers grade level spans rather than precise grade levels or ages of students. This approach allows the teacher and student greater flexibility in learning science through inquiry than an approach that denotes a multitude of discrete elements of content.

The chapter also maps out broadly what students should be given the opportunity to learn from kindergarten through high school. For those whose teaching domain is the intermediate elementary years, it should prove helpful to you to see what knowledge students ought to arrive with in your classroom, as well as what knowledge they will need as they move into middle school and high school. Secondary teachers, in the same way, will benefit from knowing the nature of the content elementary students should be exposed to as preparation for middle school and secondary science. Depending on the nature of the course you are taking, your instructor may wish to emphasize one area of science content over another.

TABLE 4.1   Changing Emphases for Content Standards*

Less Emphasis On	More Emphasis On
Knowing scientific facts and information	Understanding scientific concepts and developing abilities of inquiry
Studying subject matter disciplines (physical, life, earth sciences) for their own sake	Learning subject matter disciplines in the context of inquiry, technology, science in personal and social perspectives, and the history and nature of science
Separating science knowledge and science process	Integrating all aspects of science content
Covering many science topics	Studying a few fundamental science concepts
Implementing inquiry as a set of processes	Implementing inquiry as instructional strategies, abilities, and ideas to be learned

*Reprinted with permission from *National Science Education Standards* © 1996 by the National Academy of Sciences, courtesy of the National Academies Press, Washington, DC, p. 113.

Learning science in an integrated and interdisciplinary fashion lends itself to a deeper understanding of science in general, emphasizing the similarities in thinking and processes present among the disciplines of science. This integrated and interdisciplinary approach is supported by instructional models that promote genuine, student-driven inquiry, advocated by proponents of Science-Technology-Society (STS) approaches to teaching and learning.

An interdisciplinary approach to teaching science, as used here, refers to the application and use of knowledge and skills from across one or more intellectual domains. As such, the STS approach is interdisciplinary by its very conception. Student-generated inquiry in a real-world context drives the instruction, the science content to be learned, and the process skills to be employed. Knowledge is then developed within a real-world context, consistent with the findings of many science educators, most especially by the American Association for the Advancement of Science (1989) in *Science For All Americans*.

Yager and Penick (1991) also address the context issue. In a study they conducted, teachers revealed that the learning of science content within a realistic, student-derived context had a number of advantages, chief among these were the genuine interdisciplinary nature of the program and the increased interest on the part of both students and teachers.

Henning and King (2005) similarly report on interdisciplinary experiences in elementary classrooms via an STS approach. They cite an example of interdisciplinary instruction and problem solving of this sort with fifth grade students that was characterized by a deep connection among the areas of the content and that had been organized at a conceptual level; it also offered an excellent opportunity for social action to demonstrate the student's mastery of science and social studies content. The unit culminated in a visit from the community park district director, which allowed the fifth grade students to offer input based on their study of social and physical geography, transportation issues, and their understanding of the values in the community. They wrote a report that helped to inform the development of a new recreation area within their community.

The fundamental theme that informs the National Science Education Standards is inquiry, whether conducted in an interdisciplinary framework or in a more discipline-specific approach. This evolution in the way science should be carried out in the classroom seeks to make the focus of the science experience in America's schools more consistent with the practices of scientists in the field. Skills such as analyzing scientific information, conducting investigations over a long period of time, and using process skills in context are the beginning. Moving toward the concept of "science as argument and explanation" (National Academy of Sciences, 1996, p. 113) serves to emphasize the primacy of inquiry, critical thinking skills, and content knowledge mastery to provide the context for the skills.

Content knowledge, of course, remains the companion to inquiry in the National Science Education Standards. The desired outcome is that these two strands of engaging in science—content knowledge and the process of inquiry—will better support and complement each other. This change in the way science is conceived and delivered in the schools has far-reaching implications not only for what students learn but for how and what they are taught. Content and methods courses in universities and colleges need to prepare students not only to know scientific facts but, more importantly, how to guide students—whether primary, intermediate, or secondary—in seeking their own answers to the questions they pose.

In addition to the information shared in Table 4.1, Changing Emphases for Content Standards, Table 4.2 underscores changes in *how* science is to be taught—with the preeminent focus on inquiry. The preferred emphasis for inquiry-based science teaching focuses on engaging students as if they were real scientists. Students need to investigate and analyze science questions and carry out these investigations over an extended length of time, moving away

TABLE 4.2 Changing Emphases to Promote Inquiry*

Less Emphasis On	More Emphasis On
Activities that demonstrate and verify science content	Activities that investigate and analyze science questions
Investigations confined to one class period	Investigations over extended periods of time
Process skills out of context	Process skills in context
Individual process skills, such as observation or inference	Using multiple process skills—manipulation, cognitive, procedural
Getting an answer	Using evidence and strategies for developing or revising an explanation
Science as exploration and experimentation	Science as argument and explanation
Providing answers to questions about science content	Communicating science explanations
Individuals and groups of students analyzing and synthesizing data without defending a conclusion	Groups of students often analyzing and synthesizing data after defending conclusions
Doing a few investigations in order to leave time to cover large amounts of content	Doing more investigations in order to develop understanding, ability, the value of inquiry, and knowledge of science content
Concluding inquiries with the result of the experiment	Applying the results of experiments to scientific arguments and explanations
Management of materials and equipment	Management of ideas and information
Private communication of student ideas and conclusions to teacher	Public communication of student ideas and work to classmates

*Reprinted with permission from *National Science Education Standards* © 1996 by the National Academy of Sciences, courtesy of the National Academies Press, Washington, DC, p. 113.

from a series of discrete twenty- to forty-minute science experiences. The goal is to help students use process skills in the context of the content they are learning and not to deliver them as a separate entity. Other suggested changes seek to encourage students to enter the practice of science as a debate informed by data they have gathered and analyzed themselves, arguing points of view from a perspective of knowledge and reason, and then updating and revising their findings as new data becomes available. Connecting with a larger community—beyond the classroom—is another desired experience for students. If the knowledge gathered in their investigations is worthwhile, then it stands to reason that it is worth communicating beyond their small classroom communities to the world at large.

Examining and Interpreting the Science Content Standards

Why does a teacher have to learn content? It might be suggested that teachers are experts in pedagogy more so than in content, so being an effective teacher is more about knowing how to deliver information. However, the most effective teachers not only have deep and rich content knowledge, but also understand how to organize instruction in such a way that students learn it in meaningful ways.

The purpose of the content standards chapter of the National Science Education Standards is not to dictate a national curriculum. Rather, it emphasizes that the science experiences for K–12 students need to be broad-based and that it is inappropriate to avoid topics for convenience or political expediency. Further, the standards do not break the content knowledge down into small, discrete nuggets of information that could create a "checklist" mentality: "once covered, never to be repeated." The intention is that the content be continuously revisited at higher and higher levels of sophistication. This model, advocated by Bruner (1960), ensures that the coverage of content knowledge focuses on the depth of knowledge acquired by students, preferring deep understanding of fewer major topics over superficial knowledge of many bits of information.

Combined with learning science content at greater levels of complexity as students move from early elementary years to later elementary years, they should also become active participants in the learning process. The overall thrust of the NSES—teaching through inquiry—is intended to increase student mastery of the broad unifying concepts and processes of science. This commitment to broad concepts and principles, such as *systems, order, and organization* and *evidence, models, and explanation*, unifies the disciplines of science and provides an organizational schema that supports continued learning in science.

SCIENCE CONTENT STANDARD

As a result of activities in grades K–12, all students should develop understanding and abilities aligned with the following concepts and processes:

- systems, order, and organization
- evidence, models, and explanation
- constancy, change, and measurement
- evolution and equilibrium
- form and function

Science in the classroom operates under an umbrella of concepts, such as form and function, evolution and equilibrium, and constancy, change, and measurement, regardless of the specific discipline. Interdisciplinary approaches to teaching and learning science, such as the STS approach mentioned above, makes important use of these intellectual tools to develop instruction through real-world interdisciplinary investigations. As one of the goals of scientific literacy—that of helping individuals use their scientific knowledge for individual and public purposes—helping students to understand the common themes in science is critical. Once an individual understands the "big ideas" of science, it is a simpler proposition to add knowledge to that well-developed schema. Accommodating and assimilating new scientific information is a more manageable task if an existing framework is in place. With a comprehensive organizational plan, the student is better poised as a citizen to acquire new information and, most importantly, to understand on a systemic level the challenges and consequences of their actions in a broader context.

Defining Terms

Establishing the "big ideas" of science can be facilitated by offering concise definitions of what we are referring to when we speak of the broad concepts of science.

- ***Systems, order, and organization.*** To help scientists—and students—deal with the complexity of the natural world, smaller subsections of it—systems, for instance, may be examined. A **system** represents a group of related objects or elements that function together in a way that is both dependent and interdependent on the various parts. Living organisms, for example, represent one system; their various organs work together and independently to sustain the organism. Another example would be the solar system. It can be helpful to examine the components of the solar system—stars, planets, comets, etc.—both collectively and individually. Systems have "boundaries, components, resources flow (input and output) and feedback" (EdSTAR Minnesota, 2005a, paragraph 1).

The concept of **order** represents another fundamental tenant of science. It is an accepted scientific understanding that the world is predictable and understandable. While we do not possess an ultimate understanding of the nature of the universe, confidence in the idea that the world is knowable underlies the sense that the universe is ordered. This notion of orderliness is implicit in the laws and theories that are used to describe and explain the world. Gas laws, laws of motion and energy conservation, the principle of superposition, and laws of heredity are all examples of how the orderliness of the world can be codified and understood.

Organization promotes different ways to think about the world and how it is arranged. From the simplest efforts of a young child to rank a set of objects from tallest to shortest to a team of physicists seeking evidence for a new element, the value of ordering and seeking a means of organizing information represents another key element of scientific understanding and investigation. Examining rocks and minerals and classifying them as sedimentary, igneous, or metamorphic informs the student not only about the type of rocks he or she is investigating, but also about the effects of heat, pressure, and sedimentation, and how the changes from one rock to another infers a rock's relationship with its environment and other factors that shape its form and its history. Examining organisms from the perspective of a classification scheme can inform the learner about the relationship between an organism and other forms of life.

Evidence, models, and explanation. Just as no jury should convict a defendant without evidence to support the judgment, the development of ideas in science relies on the use of data and observations as **evidence** to support a position. One of the most important responses a teacher can give to a student may be, "That may be your conclusion, but what *evidence* do you have from your investigation to support your belief?" Justifying a point of view based on evidence is a hallmark of science, regardless of grade level and regardless of the discipline.

Models represent an explanation that "correspond[s] to real objects, events, or classes of events, and that have explanatory power" (EdSTAR Minnesota, 2005b, paragraph 3). Models can range from physical to mathematical, but in all cases they help scientists understand how something works. Many children are familiar with model trains and model cars; in much the same way that a scale model toy can represent characteristics of the real thing, so do models in science. Mathematical models can be used to examine the characteristics of systems that are too difficult or costly to examine in the laboratory. An example of the importance of computer-generated mathematical models as keys to understanding includes a recent U.S. Geologic Survey groundwater computer model that was used to inform decisions regarding the proposed Yucca Mountain nuclear waste dump. When the model was challenged, the ability to make an informed decision to construct the storage site was greatly compromised (Associated Press, 2005, March 18). While not as grave, the same mathematical approach to modeling can be developed and applied as students develop a mathematical model describing the proportion of chewing gum that is composed of sugar.

Explanation represents how students explain the use of evidence and data as they develop their understanding of scientific knowledge and processes. In science, perhaps more than any other academic discipline, *how* the answer was developed is as important as what the actual answer might be. It is expected that the explanation will make use of data and observations and express in a logical and coherent fashion how the information was used to achieve a conclusion. Also, part of the substance of explanation is the expectation that individuals will be willing to defend in an open forum their ideas and the strength of the arguments used in developing their conclusions. Furthermore,

> different terms, such as "hypothesis," "model," "law," "principle," "theory," and "paradigm" are used to describe various types of scientific explanations. As students develop and as they understand more science concepts and processes, their explanations should become more sophisticated. That is, their scientific explanations should more frequently include a rich scientific knowledge base, evidence of logic, higher levels of analysis, greater tolerance of criticism and uncertainty, and a clearer demonstration of the relationship between logic, evidence, and current knowledge. (EdSTAR Minnesota, 2005b, paragraph 5)

- *Constancy, change, and measurement.* How things remain the same and how things change are another important set of broad constructs in science. **Constancy** is evident in such fundamental principles as the conservation of matter and the conservation of energy. It also helps us to see broader cycles, that imbed local change, cycles, and processes. Noting the conservation of matter and energy, for instance, allows one to see the "bigger picture" during physical and chemical changes in matter. But **change** itself is a fundamental experience in science, whether we see it as growth in plants and animals, long-term geologic changes, movement of planets through the solar system, or electrons in a probability cloud in the vicinity of an atom's nucleus.

  Measurement allows the investigation of processes in a quantifiable manner, allowing us to track changes or note the absence of change (EdSTAR Minnesota, 2005c, paragraph 3). Concepts such as rate of change and scale are embedded in the application of measurement skills.

- *Evolution and equilibrium.* These terms represent the "yin and yang" of science concepts, as changes are compared and contrasted with the balance between and among competing elements of systems as they seek to preserve equilibrium. **Evolution** is commonly associated with biological evolutions—changes in organisms over time— and this provides an excellent example of the broader meaning of the concept. Changes in the universe, both sporadic and gradual, bring us to our present configuration of the state of things and give us the ability to see and make predictions about changes that will take place. These changes are evidence of evolution in play (EdSTAR Minnesota, 2005d, paragraph 2). **Equilibrium** comes into play as systems work in opposition to one another; for example, osmosis and diffusion represent examples of systems reaching equal concentrations of water or another substance throughout an entire system. Other examples may be noted when forces of equal magnitude and opposite in direction are applied to each other in opposition, which prevents movement of the system (EdSTAR Minnesota, 2005d, paragraph 3).

- *Form and function.* Architect Louis Sullivan used these terms: "form follows from function." In the same way, our concepts of form and function in science operate in a similar fashion, with form and function influencing each other in mutually interdependent ways. The **function** of an object or a system can often be inferred from the **form** it takes; the filaments in a fish's gills, as an example, allow oxygenated water flowing past the gill structure to let dissolved oxygen enter the bloodstream of the fish.

Content Standard A

The standards of scientific inquiry move beyond previous curricular approaches that taught science process skills in isolation. The intention of Content Standard A is that students will develop and refine their ability to learn science by actually engaging in acts of scientific inquiry. Beyond simply learning about the skills, students will be challenged to *use* the skills as they engage in school science experiences.

What science is has been revealed numerous times by what students share on the classic "Draw a scientist activity." When asked to sketch a scientist, many students will create a stereotypical image of a scientist (white male, surrounded by icons of scientific knowledge, evidence of social ineptitude) that is consistent with their naïve notions of what it is to actually engage in science. This provides evidence of obstacles to learning science through inquiry, as the focus of science is demonstrated by student drawings as a task most consistently done by white males in lab coats and only when surrounded by iconic symbols of science: test tubes, beakers, Bunsen burners, and the like.

> **CONTENT STANDARD A: SCIENCE AS INQUIRY**
>
> As a result of activities in grades K–12, all students should develop
>
> - abilities necessary to do scientific inquiry
> - understanding about scientific inquiry

These stereotypical images of what a scientist looks like tend to be consistent with inexperienced understandings of how science is conducted. Unfortunately, these images tend to be embedded as early as fourth or fifth grade and do not change without specific instruction (Finson, Beaver, & Cramond, 1995). The drawings of scientists do not include the action of learning science content through inquiry. Addressing naïve conceptions of science requires addressing not only the content, but also helping students learn the context of the nature of science and scientific inquiry (Gess-Newsome, 2002). Explicit teaching of scientific inquiry and the nature of science is necessary for students to learn *through* scientific inquiry. This change in organizing instruction, however, begins with teachers. Luft (2001) offers persuasive evidence that teachers need to have explicit instruction in learning and teaching science through inquiry before they can begin to effectively teach their students through inquiry.

The essentials of inquiry-based science instruction are clearly delineated by Carin, Bass, and Contant (2005) through their introduction of the learning-cycle method for organizing instruction. Students are engaged by scientific questions, ideally of their own construction. The learners then devise their own investigations and seek to collect meaningful data that will allow them to answer the questions they devised at the beginning of the investigation. Based on their questions, they design and construct investigations that allow them to answer the questions they posed through the use of the data they collected during the investigation. Their findings are then connected to a broader scientific understanding through a process of critical discussion of what they learned, with particular attention paid to the use of the data they collected to support their point of view.

Presented in Lesson 4.1 is an example of a physical science investigation on the topic of friction. In the investigation, which is left open-ended, the procedure makes some suggestions as to what the students might look for as they carry out an investigation of forces that influence friction. The teacher encouraged students to explain how they used the evidence they collected to confirm or reject the ideas they investigated during their closing presentation.

SUPPORTING SCIENCE CONTENT STANDARD A: LESSON 4.1

Investigation Idea: Student Inquiry

This activity was designed by a teacher to help students develop greater autonomy in terms of designing and conducting their own investigations. This is somewhat structured, in that the investigation requires that the student make specific predictions, design an investigation to test those predictions, and then explain how the data collected supported or provided no support for the predictions the student made. Investigations such as this provide an intermediate step between teacher-directed laboratory investigations and pure open inquiry investigations.

Procedure

Use spring scales and the different types of surfaces, as well as wooden blocks of different sizes, to look for patterns in frictional forces. You should strive to be as quantitative as possible: measure the mass of the wooden blocks, measure the force on the spring scale, and measure the surface area of the blocks. With this in mind, investigate the following;

1. What happens if you double the weight by stacking one block on top of the other?
2. What happens if you keep the weight the same but double the surface area?
3. How does the type of surface affect the frictional force?

Teacher Approval

Outline your investigation, with particular attention being paid to the following points:

- What do you expect will take place?
- What sort of evidence will support your prediction?

Teacher approval: _____
                                (Teacher Initial)

Data and Calculations:

Data for Investigation 1:

Data for Investigation 2:

Data for Investigation 3:

Conclusion

Develop a concluding statement regarding friction and how each of the investigations provided evidence to support your conclusion.

    Conclusion regarding the force of friction:

- How did the data from investigation 1 inform your conclusion?
- How did the data from investigation 2 inform your conclusion?
- How did the data from investigation 3 inform your conclusion?

The investigation presented in Lesson 4.1 offers the teacher the opportunity to interact with the students before they begin their actual investigation to help them determine whether or not their investigation adequately tests—and will report—on the data in the way they believe it will. Students and teachers with more experience in learning science through inquiry may wish to minimize this step.

Note that the standards are the same at all levels, K–12: students will acquire and demonstrate the "abilities necessary to do scientific inquiry" and develop an "understanding about scientific inquiry." It is a tacit assumption of the NSES that scientific inquiry can be made meaningful and relevant for students of all ages and all levels of experience. Scientific inquiry is not something to be saved for graduate school. It is an important process of thinking and understanding that is best accomplished by creating developmentally appropriate experiences for students to actually engage in inquiry.

SUPPORTING SCIENCE CONTENT STANDARD A: LESSON 4.2

Investigation Idea: Student Inquiry

This investigation offers a method of collecting data that will determine the average acceleration of bodies falling to the earth. Despite using arbitrary "washer" units, the constant value of acceleration will be revealed through this investigation. This investigation uses a paper tape timer apparatus as a means of gathering appropriate data.

Background:

What would you predict about the movement of objects as they fall toward the earth? Write a statement in the space below sharing your thoughts on how "light" objects fall as compared to "heavy" objects:

Prediction:

Evidence:

Procedure:

1. Push the end of a length of timer tape (about 1.5 m) into the timer. With masking tape, attach either a 200 g mass or 10 metal washers. Start the timer and release the mass/washers so that it falls to the floor, pulling the tape behind it and through the timer. Mark this tape as "10 Washers" and set aside for data processing.
2. Repeat this process for 20, 30, 40, and 50 washers, in each case labeling the tape with the number of washers used during the trial.
3. Number every fifth dot and use this as your time scale. Measure the distance between each fifth dot.
4. Because you are measuring in each case the displacement of the mass during one "tock" of time, the distance and the average velocity of the mass for a given tick are numerically the same. Enter your displacement and velocity measurements in Tables 1 and 2.
5. The acceleration values may be calculated by determining the average slope of pairs of points on the acceleration time graph.
6. Plot the data on the accompanying graphs so as to produce a displacement-time, velocity-time, and acceleration-time graph.

Data and Calculations:

TABLE 1

Time (tocks)	AVERAGE VELOCITY (CM/TOCK)				
	Tape 1–10 washers	Tape 2–20 washers	Tape 3–30 washers	Tape 4–40 washers	Tape 5–50 washers
1					
2					
3					
4					
5					
6					
7					
8					
9					
10					

(continued)

TABLE 2

Number of washers	Acceleration (cm/tick^2) (average of Velocity-Time graphs)
10	
20	
30	
40	
50	

Interpretation:

Graph 1. Create a graph to represent Velocity (cm/tick) as a function of Time (ticks)

- What form do the set of points take on this graph? Is this what you would expect, based on what you know about motion? Why or why not?
- Interpret the meaning of the slope for this graph.

Graph 2. Create a graph to represent Acceleration (cm/tick^2) as a function of Mass (Number of washers)

- What form do the set of points take on this graph? Is this what you would expect, based on what you know about motion? Why or why not?
- What do the points tell us about the acceleration of objects of different masses?

Students should also, as they make inquiry in science, learn to think about the process of scientific inquiry. Learning to appreciate how science is used to find information—and its strengths and limitations—is an important part of becoming scientifically literate (Lederman & Abd-El-Khalik, 1998). Learning about the strengths *and* the limitations of science prepares students as citizens. The frequent debates that are raging in and around public schools on topics such as evolution would be well served if some of the more strident advocates of teaching creationism would simply examine what science is and how it is used to make decisions in an appropriate domain.

Content Standard B

The content standards in the physical sciences offer several implications. First and foremost, along with the skills of inquiry, physical science content knowledge is valued and should be available for all students, K–12. In the early grades, exposure and mastery of physical science concepts focuses on acquiring basic knowledge of the skills, such as their basic physical properties—solids, liquids, and gasses—as well as developing an understanding of position and movement of objects. The physical science standards for the primary grades would also introduce students to basic topics of heat, light, electricity, and magnetism. At this level, introduction and initial exposure

---

CONTENT STANDARD B: PHYSICAL SCIENCE

As a result of activities in grades K–4, all students should develop an understanding of

- the properties of object and materials
- the position and motion of objects
- light, heat, electricity, and magnetism

As a result of activities in grades 5–8, all students should develop an understanding of

- properties and changes of properties in matter
- motions and forces
- transfer of energy

As a result of activities in grades 9–12, all students should develop an understanding of

- the structure of atoms
- the structure and properties of matter
- chemical reactions
- motions and forces
- conservation of energy and increase in disorder
- interactions of energy and matter

to concepts is most appropriate. At higher levels, topics such as magnetism require an appreciation of modeling and the ability to engage in a certain amount of abstract reasoning, for instance when topics such as magnetic domains are introduced. For primary students, exposure to magnets and helping them understand basic properties such as attraction and repulsion is appropriate. Understanding the *whys* of this behavior are better served at a later point in the student's educational program.

SUPPORTING SCIENCE CONTENT STANDARD B: LESSON 4.3

Investigation Idea: Work and Kinetic Energy

For high school students, this investigation on the relationship between kinetic energy and work may be of interest.

Prediction:

Imagine a pendulum bob colliding with a stationary mass. During a collision between a pendulum bob and a block of wood, the pendulum bob does not return to its original height, due to it having transferred some of its energy to the wood block, For this investigation, consider how the work done to the wooden block compares to the energy lost by the pendulum bob. Make a prediction as to what you believe will take place, and state further what evidence will persuade you to support your prediction.

Prediction:

Evidence:

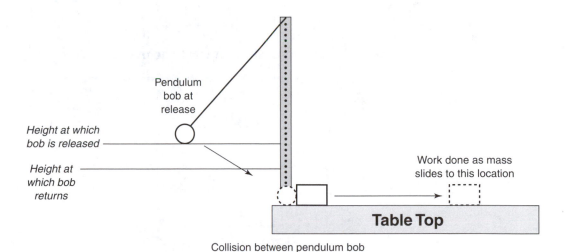

Collision between pendulum bob
and mass takes place here

Procedure:

1. Set up a pendulum, making sure that it swings freely through the entire swing and that the bottom part of the swing is close to the tabletop. You will need to know the mass of the pendulum bob(s) that you test.
2. Depending on which relationship you wish to test for, you will want to vary one factor at a time while keeping all other factors constant.
3. You will need to measure the height the bob returns to after the collision/energy transfer takes place. Use this to calculate the potential energy *after* the interaction. This will be tricky, so multiple trials will help to ensure that you get a good average value.

4. Repeat this for a number of trials, using either different masses or using different release heights for the pendulum bob.
5. Of interest will be to compare the energy input in the system (*mgh*) versus the energy/work applied to the system (F Δ x, the work done by friction bringing the block of wood to a halt after it is struck by the pendulum).
6. Variables under investigation:
   - What variable are you testing?

   - What variables must you keep constant?

   - What assumptions will you make during this investigation?

Data and Calculations:

$F_f =$ _____

(The grid here is for your convenience only. You do not need to use all of the cells. Be sure to label them with the variable and the units.)

Sample Calculations (show at least one of each):

- Potential energy calculation (before collision)

- Potential energy calculation (after collision)

- Difference between values above (1)

- Work done by block from friction (2)

- Difference between (1) and (2)

Summary:

Compose a summary statement regarding the relationships you discovered during this investigation.

Structure your response so that you include the elements outlined in the scoring rubric.

Scoring Rubric: Summary

Plentiful		
No examples from investigation 0	1 (numerical) example from investigation cited 1	2 or more (numerical) examples from investigation cited 2
Relevant		
Example(s) unrelated to conclusion 0	Example(s) marginally relates to conclusion 1	Examples clearly relate to conclusion 2
Accurate		
Evidence (data) not what one would expect to result from an investigation of this type 0	Evidence (data) generally what one would expect to result from an investigation of this type 1	Evidence (data) consistent with what one would expect to result from an investigation of this type 2
Specific		
Conclusion does not use specific example from investigation 0	Conclusion uses at least 1 specific example from lab OR 1 example drawn from text (includes specific page and citation) 1	Conclusion uses 1 specific example from lab AND 1 example drawn from text (includes specific page and citation) 2
Evidence		
Numerical evidence (data) is not used to support conclusion 0	Numerical evidence (data) is used to support conclusion in a general manner 1	Multiple pieces of numerical evidence (data) is used to support conclusion in a compelling manner 2

Score for Summary:

____/10

SUPPORTING SCIENCE CONTENT STANDARD B: LESSON 4.4

Implementation Idea: Magnets

As an example of helping students apply inquiry in learning about the physical sciences, consider the topic of magnets. Here, organizing instruction in such a way that inquiry is promoted can lead students to a better understanding of the properties of magnets. This lesson is quite suitable for elementary students.

Give students three sealed envelopes—one with a donut-shaped magnet, one with a metal washer, and one with a rubber washer inside. Mark the envelopes in some manner so that they can be distinguished from one another.

Allow students to investigate the envelopes without opening them. After an initial investigation period, provide the students with a variety of other items to aid in their investigation. These might include simple materials such as a paper clip, magnetic compass, brass fastener, screw, etc. Encourage students to find out as much as they can about the envelopes (and their contents) without opening them.

Use the activities to help students develop a simple classification system of *magnets, magnetic objects,* and *non-magnets.*

Adapted from Operation Primary Physical Science, 1994.

For elementary students, this activity might serve as an end in and of itself, assuming the instructional goal is to have students develop an understanding of the difference between magnets, magnetic materials, and non-magnets. For older students, an activity such as this might provide an introduction to a unit on magnets. The materials sealed in the envelopes force students to focus on the behaviors they observe as the envelopes interact, without immediately using their observation of the contents of the envelope to influence their responses. During a science methods class for adult students, I used the same activity and consistently found that even adults tend to make assumptions about magnets and their behaviors, unless some method is employed to focus them on the interaction between the envelopes containing the objects, rather than direct observation of the objects themselves.

The same physical science content identified as appropriate for primary grade students is also appropriate for intermediate and middle grade students. As their ability to reason and think abstractly develops during these years, the level of complexity related to understanding these concepts grows as well. Rather than simply looking at heat, light, and magnetism, now these concepts are examined through the lens of energy and how energy is transferred throughout a system. Likewise, properties of matter are still important, but understanding how matter and its properties change and how these changes are related to the transference of energy begins to take on greater significance.

By the time students are in high school, the content knowledge expected of them has grown considerably more sophisticated. From their earlier knowledge of properties of matter, which can be learned directly through observation and classification activities, students now look for evidence that supports contemporary models and ways of understanding how matter is organized and structured. The structure of atoms, to note the first content knowledge point for students in grades 9–12, becomes not only the content knowledge objective, but understanding the structure of matter as atoms and molecules helps students understand other properties of matter, such as diffusion, heat transference, and changes of state. Knowing the structure of matter and its properties can help a student understand the intricate crystal patterns that form from frost and with snowflakes as well as why the aluminum foil wrapped around a baked potato cools off immediately, while the inside of the potato remains piping hot for many minutes.

Other elements of physical science content knowledge include understanding how chemical reactions take place and what happens when they occur. Motion and force studies, knowledge of the transfer and conservation of energy, of entropy, and how matter and energy interact form several of the core experiences for secondary science students. How the coursework is organized—whether through several years of interdisciplinary science activities or through more traditional discipline-centered courses in physical science, chemistry, and physics—is up to the local school district and its culture. Most importantly, the need to deliver this content so that all students benefit from it offers the most significant challenge to the teacher.

Content Standard C

If one were to rank the "popularity" of the sciences in school, it is likely that the content related to the life sciences would be ranked number one. From the first days of kindergarten, studying apples, growing plants, observing butterflies and clouds, and trips to the school yard to observe trees and plants offer many children their first experiences in science. In the primary grades, information focuses on understanding the characteristics of living organisms—their need for food, for shelter, and to reproduce. Related fundamentally is understanding how organisms live their lives from birth to death, with reproduction in the

---

CONTENT STANDARD C: LIFE SCIENCE

As a result of activities in grades K–4, all students should develop an understanding of

- the characteristics of organisms
- the life cycles of organisms
- organisms and environments

As a result of activities in grades 5–8, all students should develop an understanding of

- the structure and function in living systems
- reproduction and heredity
- regulation and behavior
- populations and ecosystems
- diversity and adaptations of organisms

As a result of activities in grades 9–12, all students should develop an understanding of

- the cell
- the molecular basis of heredity
- biological evolution
- the interdependence of organisms
- matter, energy, and organizations in living systems
- the behavior of organisms

---

middle. Plants are ubiquitous in the primary classroom; other students have access to insects ranging from mealworms to butterflies; some classrooms have class pets. All these examples provide opportunities to observe and experience living organisms in action, and all serve as platforms for meaningful elementary science experiences.

In the intermediate grades, life science experiences move from recognition and understanding of organisms and their environments toward a deeper understanding of the parts of an organism. As students move through their science curricula during grades 5–8, they begin to branch out from their initial life science experiences. They start to learn of the structure and function of living systems and develop an understanding of reproduction and heredity in organisms. Students also learn about the regulation of biological systems and the various behaviors in which animals engage. Seeing plants, animals, and other organisms as part of a larger structure, students learn about populations and ecosystems and how diversity and adaptation of organisms have helped them survive and interact with one another.

As students enter high school, the depth of their content knowledge in the life sciences should continue to grow. As students in the intermediate grades moved from studying organisms to the systems that make up the organism, students in the secondary years examine the structures that make up the systems they studied previously: the cells. Cell theory lends itself to understanding how the molecules that make up the cells are involved in biological processes such as heredity and evolution.

SUPPORTING SCIENCE CONTENT STANDARD C: LESSON 4.5

Investigation Idea: Inheritance and Evolution

This classic investigation can be structured to support inquiry practices in life science classes. Fruit flies and the characteristics of their offspring can be used to confirm lecture-based and reading materials on heredity by using the concrete experience of mating fruit flies with different phenotypes (red-eyed and white-eyed). By comparing gender and eye color on generations of fruit flies bred in the laboratory, a model for inheritance patterns may be developed.

Student data will likely show that eye color follows a sex-linked inheritance pattern. The teacher can assist with the interpretation of this information, helping students develop the inference that the alleles for a particular trait are found either on the X or Y chromosome. In the case of fruit flies, *Drosophila melanogaster*, the allele for eye color is found on the X chromosome. The allele for red eyes, R, is dominant to the allele for white, r. A more refined appreciation of these relationships—and the proportions emerging from generation to generation—can be promoted by compiling data for an entire class or between multiple classes studying the same topic.

As a technology-based alternative, software such as the Genetics Construction Kit (http://www.bioquest.org/BQLibrary/library/gck.html) can provide another means of modeling Mendelian genetics—with multiple generations generated in seconds and no pesky fruit flies to deal with.

Concurrent with studying cells, systems, and heredity, studying organisms on a larger scale in a way that emphasizes their interdependence becomes a dominant theme in life science studies at the secondary level. Uniting the study of organisms and their interdependence is the study of how matter and energy move through the system, providing a point of intersection and organization for studying living systems on a large scale. The need for comprehensive understanding of matter and energy—science content drawn from the physical sciences—underscores the need for science instruction to be comprehensive throughout the K–12 years, as knowledge of physical science concepts becomes important when studying advanced topics in the life sciences.

CONTENT STANDARD D: EARTH AND SPACE SCIENCE

As a result of activities in grades K–4, all students should develop an understanding of

- the properties of earth materials
- objects in the sky
- changes in earth and sky

As a result of activities in grades 5–8, all students should develop an understanding of

- the structure of the earth system
- the earth's history
- the earth in the solar system

As a result of activities in grades 9–12, all students should develop an understanding of

- energy in the earth system
- geochemical cycles
- the origin and evolution of the earth system
- the origin and evolution of the universe

Content Standard D

The video *A Private Universe* (1987) explains how student misconceptions are formed and how teachers can expose these misconceptions among their students. The content knowledge used to demonstrate these naive beliefs is the basic knowledge contained in this standard: how the earth moves around the sun, how the sun moves around the earth, and what is responsible for the seasons. As seen in the video, a sample of new graduates, alumni, and faculty members of Harvard University explain the movements of the earth through a series of innocent misconceptions about the way the solar system functions. While the message of the videotape is instructional, it makes a strong point regarding the lack of quality science knowledge in general and the lack of an accurate understanding of the relationships among the earth, moon, and sun in particular. This is the important knowledge contained in Content Standard D.

SUPPORTING SCIENCE CONTENT STANDARD D: LESSON 4.6

Implementation Idea: Earth, Moon, and Stars*

An excellent opportunity to develop an appreciation for long-term inquiry among students is to collect data regarding the position of the moon and the sun as observed from earth. A good primer for this activity is the GEMS curriculum guide *Earth, Moon, and Stars* (Sneider, 1986). Sneider's work promotes an understanding of the movement of the moon and its phases in terms of how ancient peoples explained their own observations and how our contemporary civilization seeks to explain the same observations.

To support long-term inquiry, students should make daily observations for at least a month, noting the position of the sun and moon with respect to each other, measuring the distance between them by counting the number of times their fists fit between the image of the sun and the image of the moon. The number of fists provides an angular measure between these objects. In addition, the phase of the moon is recorded for each of these observations.

At the end of the observation period, students seek patterns related to the angular measure and the phase of the moon they observe. The key result here is that the smaller the angle (on either side of the sun), the smaller the phase of the moon. As the angular measure between the sun and the moon increases, the moon waxes closer and closer to a full moon.

These concepts are reinforced by the use of powerful modeling activities. In this experience, students stand in a circle around a table lamp and hold small balls that represent the moon. As students rotate in place, they can see how the illuminated side of the "moon" in their hand changes as their body rotates. In this way, they make powerful connections between the data they collected and the observations they make with the modeling experience.

---

*Adapted and modified from the Great Explorations in Math and Science (GEMS) teacher's guide entitled *Earth, Moon, and Stars.* Copyright by The Regents of the University of California.

Earth and space science make up the elements of Content Standard D. As with the other content standards, the initial experiences for students in the primary grades should be developed through the most direct means possible. Consistent with that instructional goal, the earth and space science knowledge desired for young children relates to their developing an understanding of the properties of earth materials, such as hardness, texture, and how these materials are similar and dissimilar to each other. Much of the prior knowledge students bring to school will be based on their regular interactions with the earth and earth materials. The teacher has an opportunity here to help them look more closely at what they have already experienced and understand the makeup of familiar things such as soil and rocks.

Objects in the sky—clouds, rain, the stars, and planets—are also familiar to students and offer many opportunities for close examination of their features, including how they change over time. The calendar time activity, which is omnipresent in the kindergarten classroom, is one way that science is integrated into the world of the young child. Daytime astronomy activities can alert young children to the movements of the sun across the sky and how the paths it takes from morning to night changes along with the seasons. This understanding helps students better understand the relationship between the position of the sun and the seasons as they continue to examine these experiences in the intermediate and secondary grades.

Older students are capable of a higher level of understanding as their ability to engage in abstract thought becomes more powerful. Moving beyond the "here and now," the science content appropriate for students of this age looks at the overall structure of the solar system and the patterns present among the various types of planets. Looking backward into time, a knowledge and appreciation of the earth's history—and how science is used to explain events that took place before humans could study these events—works to develop an appreciation for the explanatory power of scientific investigations. Finally, understanding the earth's place in the solar system as one of nine planets, a myriad of asteroids, and the sun, along with its movements, comprise the essential earth space content knowledge for students in grades 5–8.

By the time students enter high school, the quality of their knowledge should prepare them to be active, participating, and knowledgeable citizens, even if they do not elect to pursue an active study of science past high school. The earth and space science standards for high school students build on the knowledge that was developed previously, helping students understand the role of energy in the evolution and operation of the earth system. The properties of the earth itself are examined in terms of how the earth came to be and how it has evolved during its existence. Following the earth's origin, developing an understanding of the various cycles that have continuously shaped the earth for the last few billion years and the importance of understanding these cycles becomes an important part of this experience. Current topics within the political and scientific conversations of the day, such as whether global warming is part of a broad series of cycles continuously experienced by the earth or whether global warming is a process that has been accelerated by the burning of fossil fuels over the last hundred years, offer two sides for consideration that require an educated citizenry. Lastly, the big questions—Where did the universe begin? And how has it evolved?—offer both closure and a broad perspective to the information contained in this content standard. How life on earth is lived and the changes that humans experience—and create—form the core of Content Standard E: Science and Technology.

Content Standard E

Science and technology comprise an ever-growing field of exploration and an ever-growing content area to consider within science instruction. Based on experiences in grades K–4, students should begin to gain a sense of how science and technology complement each other. A physicist once spoke of his craft as that of an artist. Like a sculptor or a painter, he created knowledge through science for the sheer pleasure and gratification of creating this knowledge. To continue with the same metaphor, if one likens a scientist to a painter/artist, those whose area of expertise is technology are more like housepainters. Both groups employ many of the same tools, much of the same knowledge base, and use many of the same processes and procedures to obtain their goals. Whereas the pure scientist creates knowledge for the sake of creating knowledge, a housepainter—technologist— has a specific goal in mind. This is not a value judgment that one profession is greater or more worthy than the other—it is simply that they use many of the same tools but with different ends in mind.

> **CONTENT STANDARD E: SCIENCE AND TECHNOLOGY**
>
> As a result of activities in grades K–4, all students should develop
>
> - abilities of technological design
> - an understanding of science and technology
> - abilities to distinguish between natural objects and objects made by humans
>
> As a result of activities in grades 5–12, all students should develop
>
> - abilities of technological design
> - an understanding of science and technology

For the student in the primary grades, an understanding of the relevant goals and abilities of technological design starts in a simple fashion, as students begin to learn about what science and technology are—their respective strengths, purposes, and tools. Furthermore, for the purposes of younger students, developing the ability to distinguish between natural objects and human-constructed objects is a fundamental goal. While this seems obvious to adults, there are challenges for children as they learn through direct experiences with materials. A design activity for a young child can be as simple as building a small boat from aluminum foil, and learning how many paper clips various designs can hold. By manipulating the foil into different shapes, the student uses a trial and error approach to increase the capacity of the boat. The experience may then be generalized to other boat-building materials such as modeling clay. Early on, children in grades K–4 can carry out design activities before they are prepared to engage in inquiry activities, so technology studies are most appropriate (National Research Council, 1994, p. 135).

Underlying the technology content standards is the need for students, regardless of grade level, to appreciate and understand the principles of technological design and how it differs from scientific inquiry. The process of design includes:

- Identification of a problem
- Proposing a solution
- Implementing proposed solutions
- Evaluating a product or design, and
- Communicating a problem, design, and solution (National Research Council, pp. 137–138)

While the process of technological design has some similarities to practices of scientific inquiry, the focus on achieving a solution as opposed to seeking knowledge is a key difference; this is an appreciation that needs to be developed in students.

 Try This! 4–1 *Technological Design*

SUPPORTING SCIENCE CONTENT STANDARD E

There are a variety of experiences that can be developed for classroom use, simply based on the everyday lives of students. As one simple example, a challenge proposed by the author during his tenure as a high school physics teacher was to have his students develop a means of keeping the water in a dog dish from freezing. A variety of solutions emerged from the experience, some expected (placing a heating coil in the water), others less so. In one memorable example, the student placed a magnet underneath the water dish, with the magnet attached to a slowly moving gear. A large bearing in the water dish moved as the magnet pulled it along, providing sufficient agitation to the water to keep it from freezing.

More materials have been developed in this area recently. The National Science Teachers Association sponsored the development of several curriculum packages that employ technological design experiences to develop science content knowledge. In *Construct a Glove* (Pulis, 2000), students take on the challenge of developing an efficient and cost-effective glove, which helps students develop a deeper understanding of concepts of thermodynamics as they construct and test their glove models.

In similar ways, *Construct a Boat* (Baroway, 2000) and *Construct a Greenhouse* (Lee, 2000) help students develop knowledge of optics, heat transfer, and buoyancy, while solving a real-world problem.

Older students—grades 5–8—should have the opportunity to develop similar expertise. By the time students are in grade 5, distinguishing between natural and man-made materials has ceased to be an issue, while their ability to engage in more sophisticated technological design experiences has grown. At the same time, students' growing appreciation for the issues related to technological design and technological solutions to problems needs to be developed, as they see more and more how technology influences their lives. Appreciating the consequences of technological solutions, how tools are used to acquire information, and how people collaborate as they pursue answers to questions are all a part of this standard. In addition, an understanding of the reciprocal nature of technology and science is developed during this time. The facts that scientific investigations drive technological innovations and advances in technology support investigations in science are part of an overall appreciation for the role of science and technology.

High school age students further refine their understanding of science and technology issues. Students at the high school level learn about the relative strengths of science and technology, and how they complement each other. Learning the constraints each operates under helps the student to learn when problems are best approached through a "scientific lens" or through a technological one. The challenges a teacher faces in meeting this standard is stated well in the NSES:

> The choice of design tasks and related learning tasks is an important and difficult part of addressing this standard. In choosing technological learning

activities, teachers of science will have to bear in mind some important issues. For example, whether to involve the students in a full or partial design problem or whether to engage them in meeting a need through technology or studying the technological work of others. Another issue is how to select a task that brings out the various ways in which science and technology interact, providing a basis for reflection on the nature of technology while learning the science concepts involved. (p. 191)

The challenge of delivering technological design content within the framework of science coursework is a real challenge. This challenge can be met when the science curriculum in a school district is mapped out in detail, allowing for meaningful experiences in technology and science to support each other, rather than being constructed in an "add on" fashion.

Technology can represent the interface between science and the human experience. Looking at science and technology and how they interact with the individual in personal and social ways represents the intent of Content Standard F.

Content Standard F

The substance of this standard, Science in Personal and Social Perspectives, forms the third segment of the Science-Technology-Society triangle. As with the technology-related concepts, these issues serve also as conceptual organizers and specific areas of content. In addition, these concepts further serve as fundamental understandings and implied actions for most contemporary issues. The organizing principles apply to local as well as global phenomena and represent challenges that occur on scales that vary from the very short—for example, natural hazards—to very long—for example, the potential result of global changes. (National Research Council, p. 193)

In the primary grades, the focus on science issues related to personal and social perspectives begins with an emphasis on personal qualities. Studying personal health is an ideal place to begin learning about the human body and how it functions. The definition of biology for young children is related in large part to stimulating interest and wonder on the part of the young child. Applying their own natural curiosity about their bodies and allowing them to build theories and explain their observations can be extended to observing the characteristics and changes in populations (Chaillé & Britain, 1991). Recognizing that human beings are part of the environment and that the population of human beings can increase or decrease as a result of external factors, such as disease or famine, helps relate this understanding to that of populations of other species.

Young children also need to start developing an understanding of the types of resources that we make use of in our daily lives. These resources include both living and nonliving materials. In many cases these resources are finite; children need to understand that some resources are renewable, while others are limited in quantity. Setting up a classroom terrarium or aquarium can provide instructional opportunities—especially if students contribute to its construction—that

---

CONTENT STANDARD F: SCIENCE IN PERSONAL AND SOCIAL PERSPECTIVES

As a result of activities in grades K–4, all students should develop an understanding of

- personal health
- characteristics and changes in populations
- types of resources
- changes in environments
- science and technology in local challenges

As a result of activities in grades 5–8, all students should develop an understanding of

- personal health
- populations, resources, and environments
- natural hazards
- risks and benefits
- science and technology in society

As a result of activities in grades 9–12, all students should develop an understanding of

- population and community health
- population growth
- natural resources
- environmental quality
- natural and human-induced hazards
- science and technology in local, national, and global challenges

get at the very essence of what is necessary for an ecosystem to survive and prosper (Donowitz & Robbins, 1999).

Related to their understanding of natural resources is developing an appreciation for intangible qualities, such as isolation and solitude. These qualities are often threatened as we seek to harvest material resources.

A key area of understanding regarding environments is to help younger students appreciate that changes in the environment can be brought about by either natural or man-made causes. This allows the opportunity to connect this area of earth sciences with an appreciation for personal and social issues.

Beyond the personal appreciate for environmental changes and the nature of natural resources, teachers may help students in grades K–4 begin to recognize the science and technology issues embedded in local challenges. Just as there are challenges associated with acquiring limited resources, students also need to appreciate that as new technologies are developed and implemented, they often have unforeseen and unfortunate consequences. Automobiles, for instance, allow people to live farther away from their place of employment, yet time spent commuting takes people away from their families and often produces air pollution and road congestion.

SUPPORTING SCIENCE CONTENT STANDARD F: LESSON 4.7

Investigation Idea: Science–Technology–Society

An example of examining issues of science and technology in human and social perspectives can be drawn from a group of fifth grade students in the Glen Ellyn, Illinois, public schools. As part of an interdisciplinary experience examining transportation as a technological tool, they studied the history of their community and the influence of the transportation technology of the railroad on their community. (Glen Ellyn is located approximately twenty miles west of Chicago along an early rail line; it developed in large part as a commuter community serviced by the railroad.)

During their investigation of transportation issues, they learned that as Glen Ellyn became a more popular place to live, the transportation system that helped the community grow in the first place (the railroads) was aided and abetted by additional transportation infrastructures (streets and roads with fairly severe road congestion). In addition to looking at issues in developing more efficient transportation approaches in the community, they also identified ways to improve the quality of life in the community, which culminated in a presentation of their findings before the local parks administrative body that offered suggestions based on their data collection and analysis as to where new parks in the community might be appropriately located.

Intermediate students are also concerned with the same topics as primary students—science in personal and social perspectives—and, as noted before, they have the opportunity to consider them at a greater level of sophistication. One of the key obligations of the teacher at this point is to challenge children of this age, since

> students can study environmental issues of a large and abstract nature, for example, acid rain or global ozone depletion. However, teachers should challenge several important misconceptions, such as anything natural is not a pollutant, oceans are limitless resources, and humans are indestructible as a species. (p. 167)

Studying personal health issues offers an opportunity to use inquiry skills to become more aware of long term health and fitness issues. Examining "real" data on smoking, drug use, and other risk-intensive behaviors helps students to make connections between the science class experience and the world beyond the school's walls. As social pressures increase among this age group, helping them to recognize the particular dangers of behaviors such as smoking, drug

✔ Try This! 4–2 *Implementation Idea*

SUPPORTING SCIENCE CONTENT STANDARD F

A great resource for developing an understanding of humans and their connection with the environment can be found in *Project WET. Project WET* focuses on the use of water resources:

- Water moves through living and nonliving systems and binds them together in a complex web of life.
- Water of sufficient quality and quantity is important for all water uses.
- Sustainable water management is crucial for providing tomorrow's children with social and economic stability in a healthy environment.
- Awareness of and respect for water resources can encourage a personal, lifelong commitment of responsibility and positive community participation.

(Watercourse and Council for Environmental Education, 1995, p. 1)

The various activities in *Project Wet* help students gain an understanding of and a deeper appreciation for the importance of making wise choices in using water. The focus on the sustainability of water and water as an ultimately limited resources goes to the heart of Science in Personal and Social Perspectives. For more information about *Project WET*, visit http://www.projectwet.org/.

Other related projects, such as Project Wild, Learning Tree, and Wild Aquatic, offer similar approaches and teacher-ready curricula for animal life, plant life, and aquatic life, respectively.

use, and poor diet choices can serve to connect the content with the daily experiences of students.

Knowledge of populations, resources, and environments should be extended to develop knowledge introduced during the early elementary years. In particular, emphasizing the effects of overpopulation and the consequent degradation in environmental quality is an area to be emphasized. Helping students understand that "environmental degradation and resource depletion vary from region to region and country to country" also represents an essential task connected with this standard National Academy of Science, 1996 (p. 168).

Interest in natural hazards is a topic that consistently intrigues children. Understanding that natural hazards vary from location to location is important, as is understanding that human interactions with the environment may accelerate the action of some natural hazards.

It should also be understood that there are profound social and personal challenges related to the misidentification of hazards; the rate of change that is taking place has the potential to undermine or negate social responses to the change. As may be noted in the media, differences in scientific opinion on topics such as global warming can produce responses such as "the jury is still out" by political leaders. Stalling the study of topics halts what may be essential and timely action on them, which could lead to the detriment of many living things.

Middle school students may start to engage in analyzing the risks and benefits of exposing people to particular hazards. Introducing the tools of probability and statistics is appropriate during the middle school years, and using these tools along with appropriate data can help students understand the risks and benefits of both individual and group behaviors, ranging from understanding risks associated with smoking and poor diet, as well as placing a community in a flood plain.

Examining and appreciating the respective roles of science and technology in society creates fruitful discussion and debate for middle school students. Examining issues from the perspectives of science opens up students to an observation-driven view of the world. Learning how scientists acquire and evaluate information is one of the essential skills of scientific inquiry. Using these skills to examine issues in a community further strengthens the connection between classroom and community. It should also be recognized that "the effect of science on society is neither entirely beneficial nor entirely detrimental" (p. 169).

While the effects of science on society may be debated, it is also clear that society makes demands upon science, asking it to investigate and seek solutions for the challenges that society faces.

The ethics of scientific and technological decision-making are not often appreciated by the public at large. Rather than the stereotypical "mad scientist," actual scientists pay close attention to the rights of individuals—including animals—involved in research and show concern for how research may affect the larger community.

Despite the concern for humanity, scientists also recognize they do not have all the answers to the questions people are asking. Knowing the limits of science—and all types of knowledge—is a realization that students need to begin to appreciate and take into consideration as they begin to ask and seek answers to more sophisticated questions.

By the time students enter grades 9–12, their understanding of the points currently under discussion should develop a greater degree of sophistication. They should understand more fully how science and society complement each other and how they could participate in a community dialog regarding science and society. As stated succinctly in the standards, "the organizing principles apply to local as well as global phenomenon" (p. 193).

Understanding issues related to population and community health can strengthen the connection between local and global experiences that students need to develop. As an example, how communities take care of waste depends in primarily on the resources available in the community. According to United Nations Environmental Programme statistics, the population of urban centers has grown from 30% of the world's population living in cities in 1950 to over 60% today (United Nations Environmental Programme, 2005). In developed nations, the urban population is typically over 75%. In less developed nations, the urban population is increasingly in slums, where waste is essentially discarded where it is created, adding to the health issues in those communities. Today's students will have the responsibility of dealing with these issues as the movement toward sustainability and ecologically sensitive management of waste is addressed in all human communities.

A variety of related topics add further depth to this standard. Understanding sexuality, for instance, includes not only understanding anatomical structures and the biology associated with them, but also the related issues of ethics, morality, technology, and religion.

Population growth for both humans and animal species are subject to the same limiting factors: resources such as food and water, available space, and predation and disease. However, humans have the ability, through technology, to influence the relationship between themselves and the environment that supports them. These changes have brought about profound changes to local ecosystems and on a planet-wide scale as well, with the influence of pollution and production of greenhouse gases. What students learn during their science class experiences as students will influence the policy decisions that they will support or reject as citizens. How political bodies will respond to issues such as population growth, pollution, and energy requires an informed community.

An understanding of natural and human-induced hazards also helps students develop a deeper appreciation for the manner in which humans and their environment interact. As humans have developed a more technologically sophisticated existence, they have become simultaneously more and less susceptible to changes in the natural environment. They are less susceptible because technology and human-created environments insulate individuals from the natural environment; they are more susceptible because as humans have come to depend more on technology, they are less well equipped to respond as individuals to environmental changes.

The challenges that science and technology present on a local, national, and global scale inform many of the issues and concepts present in this content strand. The intellectual core of this content standard is developed most fully as students understand that science and technology must be used to inform debates on how people wish to live and how they interact socially, economically, and politically.

The astute teacher will help students engage in thoughtful civic discourse and assist students by promoting and modeling practices of positive social action. In this way, scientific and technological knowledge will be used as a tool to support personal and social action.

Content Standard G

The history and nature of science composes Content Standard G. The knowledge implied in this standard is that students can be shown that they, too, may engage in science. In the early elementary grades, students should begin to understand that science has been practiced and used by many individuals over many years. Despite this, much remains to be discovered, and members of their own class may contribute to the development of scientific knowledge.

The initial understanding of science as a human experience should be further developed during the intermediate and middle school years. Helping students understand that science makes use of many different skills becomes important, including such divergent skills as imagination and creativity. Understanding other abstract skills—often referred to as "habits of mind"—such as tenacity, perseverance, "intellectual honesty, tolerance of ambiguity, skepticism and openness to new ideas" (NSES, p. 170) further helps the student appreciate the dynamism of science. Habits of mind represent skills that help students become more self-reflective and regulated (Marzano, 1992). The American Association for the Advancement of Science (AAAS) in *Science for All Americans* uses this term to describe the intellectual tools that support independent, self-directed learning of science by students.

Some teachers approach teaching the nature of science as though it were a simple rubric of steps to be taken to get an answer or solve a problem. While these customary steps are often present as scientists consider new problems and new challenges, there also is the understanding—not often prevalent in "cookbook" science experiences—of the tentativeness of knowledge. While this is sometimes considered a critique of science by the general public (captured by a dismissive, "it's only a theory"), this tentativeness is a fundamental strength of the way

---

CONTENT STANDARD G: HISTORY AND NATURE OF SCIENCE

As a result of activities in grades K–4, all students should develop an understanding of

- science as a human endeavor

As a result of activities in grades 5–8, all students should develop an understanding of

- science as a human endeavor
- the nature of science
- the history of science

As a result of activities in grades 9–12, all students should develop an understanding of

- science as a human endeavor
- the nature of scientific inquiry
- historical perspectives

science is performed. As tentativeness gives way to greater and greater certainty, the ideas tested and vetted by many scientists over time eventually offer conclusions that are accepted by the vast majority of all scientists active in a given field.

Though scientists may disagree with an interpretation given to a set of data, *all* scientists are in agreement that testing, questioning, and open debate of ideas are a fundamental part of the scientific experience.

The scientists who develop new knowledge and new explanations today are part of an ongoing tradition of thinkers and creators of knowledge. Understanding the history of science helps students understand not only where knowledge comes from, but the great difficulties scientists encountered as they developed new knowledge. Understanding the societal issues of how and why

 Try This! 4–3 *The History of Science: Astronomy*

SUPPORTING SCIENCE CONTENT STANDARD G

The history of ideas in astronomy offers one approach for looking at how scientific ideas evolve and absorb previous ideas and how the development of science is a function of individuals and the times in which they live.

Some of the highlights are captured in the table below, which offers an excellent example of the self-correcting and evolving nature of science.

Scientist/Philosopher	Key Elements of Model	Changes from Previous Model	Notes
Ptolemy	Geocentric Circular orbits Epicycles to account for retrograde motion		
Copernicus	Heliocentric Circular orbits	Heliocentric model accounts for retrograde motion	Conflicts develop between Copernicus's cosmology and Christian theology
Brahe	Revised geocentric model	Returned earth to center of solar system, but planets orbit sun	Excellent observational astronomer Extraordinarily high level of precision
Kepler	Heliocentric model	Elliptical orbits with sun at one focus Found mathematical descriptions for movement of planets Accepting elliptical orbit for planets eliminated the need for epicycles	"Modern" scientist in the sense that he was willing to use his (Brahe's) data to support the model he developed, even though he was forced to abandon a cherished model (circular orbits for planets) Was not interested in an explanation of why his mathematical models functioned

(continued)

Scientist/Philosopher	Key Elements of Model	Changes from Previous Model	Notes
Galileo	Heliocentric	Model acquires more support through observational data	Applied observational evidence to support heliocentric model: ■ Jupiter as a center of motion (observed 4 major satellites of Jupiter; correctly inferred their motion) ■ Observed phases of Venus; correctly surmised that this combination of shadow/light would only be observed if Venus was between Earth and Sun Profound difficulties with church authorities for promoting heliocentric model
Newton	Heliocentric	Model becomes further refined as Newton develops laws of universal gravitation	Had profound physical/mathematical insight Recognizes that Kepler's laws of motion represent motion of planetary bodies based on an inverse-square relationship between force and distance; generalizes force to explain motion of all celestial bodies

decisions were made—and the strong influence of culture on the development of scientific knowledge—underscores just how profound the connection is between science and society.

By the time students are enrolled in grades 9–12, they should continue to develop their understanding of science as a human endeavor. Both the simplicity and the complexity of carrying out scientific investigations should be appreciated by students at this level.

In addition, emphasizing the ethical values of conducting science is a key element of understanding the human traditions of conducting science. As stated in the Standards:

> Scientists value peer review, truthful reporting about the methods and outcomes of investigations, and making public the results of work. Violations of such norms do occur, but scientists responsible for such violations are censured by their peers. (pp. 200–201)

Learning to appreciate and apply these skills will help students understand the core human experience of what it takes to engage in scientific inquiry.

Scientific inquiry relies on the understanding and application of basic principles: scientific investigation is founded on the use of empirical data, rigorous analysis of information, logical arguments, and seeking the best possible explanation for the data collected. All scientific ideas require observations and experiments to confirm them. Some scientific knowledge is fairly complete—large-scale changes would not be expected. Other elements of scientific knowledge are much more tentative, and the opportunity to contribute significantly to growth in these areas continues (NSES, 1996).

Looking at science from a historical perspective helps students appreciate the challenges associated with gaining knowledge. Appreciating that scientific ideas may have a different genesis, depending on the cultures that produced them, helps students appreciate the diversity of knowledge and experience in science. The worldwide practices of science and technology have contributed to changes in many nations, particularly regarding the benefits and challenges of industrialization.

Implications for Practice

The challenge of summarizing the most appropriate science content knowledge for K–12 students into a single chapter is not only daunting—it is foolhardy. It is hoped that the brief survey of each of the content areas will give you an opportunity to see broad themes and understand that they all are necessary for a coherent science program to be in place. You can further develop the ideas you have less personal knowledge of by examining books and other resources that attempt to map out the broad themes of science content. A small gem such as *Science Content for Elementary and Middle School Teachers* (Fritzer & Bristor, 2004) is obviously helpful for elementary and middle school teachers, but it is also helpful for secondary teachers who wish to broaden their content-specific knowledge to other branches of science.

The final areas of the content standards seek to connect learning science to the broader culture. This approach has many elements in common with Science-Technology-Society curriculum approaches. A theoretical and practical appreciation for this approach can be found in sources such as Bybee (1997), Kumar and Chubin (2000), and Yager (1996).

In terms of practice, the fundamental idea of this chapter is that inquiry must be present as the driving intellectual and instructional tool in science education. Inquiry will vary in sophistication from grade level to grade level, but the core experience of students asking questions and seeking answers to those questions can be made meaningful at all levels of the curriculum—and connect meaningfully with the standards (Llewellyn, 2002; National Research Council, 2000).

CLASSROOM SNAPSHOTS

NSES-Informed Development of Content Standards

By the end of his junior year in high school, Carl felt that he had recovered from his freshman year biology class. As a junior, he had taken physics from Ms. Brown. Ms. Brown's class was completely different from Mr. Beebe's class. Although, upon reflection, he had learned a lot during his freshman year biology class, it was a pretty painful experience.

In physics, the textbooks were on the shelves in the back of the room, along with other text resources and a few computers. Students used the books regularly as a resource, but they were not Ms. Brown's main teaching tool.

Each quarter during the school year the students had a "big question" to investigate. Teams of students met together, asked questions to support and clarify the big question, and worked independently. Ms. Brown tended not to lecture, but instead worked with groups of students. During her student meetings, she helped them frame their questions, develop their investigations, and assessed what they were learning.

(continued)

At the end of the quarter, the class held a conference in which they presented their results, debated their findings, and sought a common understanding. From time to time, Ms. Brown would offer a clarification of the points being made by students, but she used counter-arguments and probing questions rather than red check marks on a paper.

Carl had noticed that the class seemed to be more than simply a science class. They learned a lot of physics and tested as much of it themselves as they could. But they also learned a lot about how to work in groups with other students, how science influenced people's lives, and how to teach themselves—without exclusive reliance on a book. What he came to appreciate during his time in Ms. Brown's class was that the highest compliment she could pay to a student was not just "that's a good answer," but "that showed some good thinking."

His choices for an advanced science class to take as a senior were biology, chemistry, and physics. It was clear to him that while he would learn content in any of the classes, the experience that taught him what it takes to experience science and learn the content had to be in Ms. Brown's advanced physics course. There, he would not only learn physics, but he would learn to think as well.

Summary

Science content knowledge is readily available. Every textbook published for K–12 students is crammed full of valuable knowledge and useful information. The challenge for you as a teacher will be to deliver this knowledge in an engaging and meaningful way—and not allow a content-only monopoly take over the classroom. In science, *how* we know things is ultimately as important as *what* we know.

Science as a discipline is often considered to be composed of process skills and content knowledge. This chapter presented a summary the content knowledge appropriate for K–12 students. It should be recognized that no single chapter in a single book will provide all factual knowledge required for K–12 students, but the attempt here was to present an overview of relevant knowledge.

- Science knowledge should be focused on understanding scientific knowledge and using it in support of inquiry, should be organized within the context of inquiry, social perspectives, and the history and nature of science

- Science knowledge should be integrated with process skills, and should focus on a few fundamental ideas rather than a large number of individual facts

- Science activities should promote inquiry as a primary instructional vehicle

- The broad themes of systems/order/organization, evidence/models/explanation, constancy and change, form and function, and evolution and equilibrium should be used to demonstrate common elements throughout all science content knowledge

- Students should have the opportunity to study rich content knowledge drawn from physical science, life science, earth systems, science and technology, and science in personal and social perspectives.

References

American Association for the Advancement of Science. (1989). *Science for all Americans*. New York: Oxford University Press.

Annenburg Foundation. (1987). *A private universe*. [videotape].

Associated Press. (2005, March 18). Scientist may have falsified Yucca papers. *The New York Times.* Retrieved March 19, 2005, from http://www.nytimes.com/aponline/national/AP-Yucca-Mountain.html

Baroway, W. (2000). *Construct a boat.* Arlington, VA: National Science Teachers Association.

Bruner, J. S. (1960). *The process of education.* New York: Vintage.

Bybee, R. W. (1997). *Achieving scientific literacy.* Portsmouth, NH: Heinemann.

Carin, A. A., Bass, J. E., & Contant, T. L. (2005). *Methods for teaching science as inquiry.* Upper Saddle River, NJ: Pearson/Merrill/Prentice Hall.

Chaillé, C. & Britain, L. (1991). *The young child as scientist.* New York: HarperCollins.

Donowitz, R. & Robbins, D. (1999). The aquarium as a soggy tool: The saga of the soggy pedagogue. Retrieved on March 30, 2006, from http://www.reefs.org/library/talklog/r_donowitz_&_d_robbins_021400.html

EdSTAR Minnesota. (2005a). Science themes: Systems, order, and organization. Retrieved on March 18, 2005, from http://edstar.ncrel.org/mn/Theme.asp?ThemeID=76

EdSTAR Minnesota. (2005b). Science themes: Evidence, models, and explanation. Retrieved on March 18, 2005, from http://edstar.ncrel.org/mn/ Theme.asp?ThemeID=73

EdSTAR Minnesota. (2005c). Science themes: Constancy, change and measurement. Retrieved March 18, 2005, from http://edstar.ncrel.org/mn/Theme.asp?ThemeID=72

EdSTAR Minnesota. (2005d). Science themes: Evolution and equilibrium. Retrieved March 18, 2005, from http://edstar.ncrel.org/mn/Theme.asp?ThemeID=74

EdSTAR Minnesota. (2005d). Science themes: Form and function. Retrieved March 18, 2005, from http://edstar.ncrel.org/mn/Theme.asp?ThemeID=75

Finson, K. D., Beaver, J. B., & Cramond, B. L. (1995). Development and Field Test of a Checklist for the Draw-A-Scientist Test. *School Science and Mathematics, 95,* 195–205.

Fritzer, P. & Bristor, V. J. (2004). *Science content for elementary and middle school teachers.* Boston: Pearson Allyn and Bacon.

Gess-Newsome, J. (2002). The use and impact of explicit instruction about the nature of science and science inquiry in an elementary science methods course. *Science & Education, 11*(1), 55–67.

Henning, M. B. & King, K. P. (2005). Implementing STS in the elementary classroom: From university courses to elementary classroom. *Bulletin of Science, Technology, and Society, 25*(3), 1–6.

Kumar, D. D. & Chubin, D. E. (2000). *Science, technology, and society: A sourcebook on research and practice.* New York: Kluwer.

Lederman, N. G. & Abd-El-Khalik, F. (1998). Avoiding denatured science: Activities that promote understandings of the nature of science. In W. F. McComas (Ed.), *The nature of science in science education: Rationales and strategies* (pp. 243–254). Dordrecht, Netherlands: Kluwer.

Lee, F. (2000). *Construct a greenhouse.* Arlington, VA: National Science Teachers Association.

Llewellyn, D. (2002). *Inquire within: Implementing inquiry-based science standards.* Thousand Oaks, CA: Corwin.

Luft, J. A. (2001). Changing inquiry practices and beliefs: The impact of an inquiry-based professional development programme on beginning and experienced secondary science teachers. *International Journal of Science Education, 23*(5), 517–534.

Marzano, R. (1992). *A different kind of classroom.* Alexandria, VA: Association for Supervision and Curriculum Development.

National Research Council. (1996). *National Science Education Standards.* Washington, DC: National Academy Press.

National Research Council. (2000). *Inquiry and the National Science Education Standards: A guide for teaching and learning.* Washington, DC: National Academy Press.

Operation Primary Physical Science. (1996). *Magnets—Workshop Leader's Guide.* Baton Rouge, LA: Department of Physics and Astronomy, Louisiana State University.

Pulis, L. (2000). *Construct a glove.* Arlington, VA: National Science Teachers Association.

Shymansky, J. A. (1989). What research says . . . about ESS, SCIS, and SAPA. *Science and Children, 27*(7), 33–35.

Shymansky, J. A. (1990). A reassessment of the effects of inquiry-based science curricula of the 60's on student performance. *Journal of Research in Science Teaching, 27*(2), 127–144.

Shymansky, J., Hedges, L., and Woodworth, G. (1990). A Reassessment of the Effects of Inquiry-Based Science Curricula of the 60's on Student Performance. *Journal of Research in Science Teaching,* 27, (2), 127–144.

Silberman, C. E. (1970). *Crisis in the classroom.* New York: Random House.

Sizer, T. (1992/1984). *Horace's compromise.* Boston: Houghton Mifflin.

Sneider, C. I. (1986). *Earth, moon, and stars.* Berkeley, CA: Lawrence Hall of Science.

United Nations Environmental Programme. (2005). Key facts about cities: Issues for the urban millennium. Retrieved June 3, 2006 from http://www.unep.org/wed/2005/english/Information_Material/facts.asp

Watercourse and Council for Environmental Education. (1995). *Project WET.* Bozeman, MT: Montana State University.

Yager, R. E. (1996). *Science technology society as reform in science education.* Albany, NY: SUNY Press.

Yager, R. E. & Penick, J. E. (1991). Using science as a connector for the reformed school curriculum. *NASSP Bulletin, 76*(547), 56–68.

Programs and Policy

Chapters 5, 6, 7, and 8 of this book serve to examine the program and policy standards. Some instructors may wish to introduce these standards for preservice teachers; others may suggest looking at these when the new teacher has started teaching.

CHAPTER 5

Standards for Science Education Programs

CLASSROOM SNAPSHOTS

Michael McKee had an interest in being a good citizen. He and his spouse had recently moved to a new community, and to support her career move, he had resigned from his former position as a science teacher. While he hoped to begin teaching science again, he decided to build a better connection with his community by volunteering to serve on the school district's curriculum committee as a community member while earning a living as a computer consultant. Hopefully, he thought, his expertise in science teaching and science curriculum would find a good home until he started a new teaching position.

His offer to serve as a community member of the curriculum council was accepted, and Michael looked forward to his first meeting the following Wednesday. An agenda arrived in advance of the meeting, and it appeared that he would be able to share some of his knowledge and background immediately, as one of the business items of the agenda was to begin an examination of the district's science curriculum.

The curriculum council meeting started promptly at 4:00 P.M. The meeting started with an introduction of Michael, and the committee chair offered her thanks to Michael for volunteering and sharing his knowledge and experiences with the committee. The meeting then moved into old business regarding a language arts textbook adoption for the high school and then, at last, to the science curriculum.

Speaking for the science curriculum subcommittee was the local high school principal. He opened by stating that the committee had met and was moving into action by aligning the high school's science curriculum with the state learning standards. The principal continued for a few more minutes, focusing exclusively on issues related to teaching science at the high school. Soon, he paused and asked if there were any questions.

"I have one," said Michael, raising his hand. "You've mentioned science curriculum issues at the high school level. Where do matters stand for the elementary and middle school grades?"

"Oh!" smiled the principal. "This is the year we adopt textbooks for the high school. We won't look at the elementary curriculum for three more years, until we have to order books again."

"Ummm . . . thank you. I see." Michael, normally articulate, was dumbfounded. The most basic lesson he had learned in a curriculum course a few years before was that the textbook was a tool to deliver the curriculum—and not the basis for deciding a curriculum. But locally, the process seemed to be inverted. The district's curriculum in science was not being regarded as one seamless entity, but in pieces defined by administrative issues that, while important, were really incidental to the process of designing and defining what it looked like to teach and learn science in the local school district.

While driving home after the meeting, Michael considered his options: to quietly resign from the committee or to stay put and try to effect some change. After all, he was introduced at the meeting as a new member with some special expertise. By the time he had reached home twenty minutes later, Michael was ready to see if he could support some small measure of educational change

Introduction

It's likely that none of you, as preservice teachers, have had the opportunity to sit in as a member of a school district committee. The vignette above happened to a colleague of the author several years ago, even after the development and dissemination of the National Science Education Standards had taken place. The names, of course, have been changed to preserve the anonymity of all parties. The experience that it represents, unfortunately, remains a very common practice.

The goal of this chapter is to help you gain an appreciation for the value in developing science programs as a comprehensive "whole" and how the development of science programs for PK–12 students serves not only the needs of students, but supports professional development for teachers and the development of appropriate assessment practices for all students.

Changing Emphases

The opening story offered a number of points that might be considered examples of traditional program development practices. While the changes in emphasis noted below are not necessarily organized by priority, it is interesting to note that the desire to decrease emphasis on developing science curricula by grade levels was most evident during the curriculum council meeting vignette.

The second issue explicitly addressed in the vignette was the issue of textbook selection driving the curriculum. While the selection of appropriate books is an important issue, it is not the one that should explicitly drive the development of the curriculum.

A final point to be made from the story is the preeminent role of the principal in the curriculum development process. While principals are often defined as instructional leaders and have an overall responsibility for the implementation

TABLE 5.1   Changing Emphases for Program Standards*

Less Emphasis On	More Emphasis On
Developing science programs at different grade levels independently of one another	Coordinating the development of a K–12 science program across grade levels
Using assessments unrelated to curriculum and teaching	Aligning curriculum, teaching, and assessment
Maintaining current resource allocations for books	Allocating resources necessary for hands-on inquiry teaching aligned with the Standards
Textbook- and lecture-driven curriculum	Curriculum that supports the Standards and includes a variety of components, such as laboratories emphasizing inquiry and field trips
Broad coverage of unconnected factual information	Curriculum that includes science-related social issues that students encounter in everyday life
Treating science as a subject isolated from other school subjects	Connecting science to other school subjects, such as mathematics and social studies
Science learning opportunities that favor one group of students	Providing challenging opportunities for all students to learn science
Limiting hiring decisions to the administration	Involving successful teachers in the hiring process
Maintaining the isolation of teachers	Treating teachers as professionals whose work requires continual opportunities for learning and networking
Supporting competition	Promoting collegiality among teams to improve the school
Teachers as followers	Teachers as decision makers

*Reprinted with permission from *National Science Education Standards* © 1996 by the National Academy of Sciences, courtesy of the National Academies Press, Washington, DC, p. 224.

of a school district's curriculum in his or her school, being an administrator does not make one (necessarily) an expert in science curriculum. Teachers at all levels of the district have expertise in science content and pedagogy and need to be involved in the development and implementation of a district's science curriculum.

The important ideas captured in Table 5.1 are consistent with trends identified previously in this book and in the NSES. Among them, involving teachers as individuals with a professional investment in program development and recognizing that they are individuals with professional expertise is fundamentally important. Moving teachers to a decision-making role so that their expertise is recognized and applied helps teachers become invested in the process of program development—and the changes that accompany such a process. Fullan (1991; Massell, 1994) has noted the need for genuine teacher participation and consensus in programmatic and curricular change. Regarding science education, Alberts and Heyman (1997) develop and articulate exactly the same points: teachers need to be fundamentally involved in the conception, design, and implementation of their district's science curriculum.

The involvement of teachers and a change in thinking about curriculum and science programs are only two elements of the necessary changes for science education programs. The broadly stated changes in emphases for science education programs are described above and specific markers for progress are described below. We will examine five specific elements for science education program standards.

Examining and Interpreting the Science Education Program Standards

What does a science program look like? How should it meet the needs of students? How should it be developed? How should it be implemented? The program standards for science education outline the key fundamental issues to strive for as science programs evolve.

Program Standard A

An effective science program requires planning on many levels. First and foremost, a set of clearly articulated goals is essential, as they serve to provide direction for the development of science education programming. These goals will provide the purpose around which the design of the program, the curriculum, and other science experiences—such as assessment—are developed. The curriculum should have a well-designed and well-articulated framework with specific content goals, inquiry goals, and process skills in place to support inquiry across the entire school experience.

As a companion to the curriculum, instructional practices need to be codified so that the methods employed are consistent with calls for inquiry-based practices. Current texts in science methods courses reflect the goal of teaching science through inquiry (Abruscato, 2000; Carin & Bass, 2001; Etheredge & Rudnitsky, 2003; Krajcik, Czerniak, & Berger, 1999).

While this has been discussed in some detail in a previous chapter, "assessment policies and practices should be aligned with the goals, student expectations, and curriculum frameworks" (NAS, 1996, p 210 p. 210). Student learning experiences—whether content, instruction, or assessment—should not be developed in isolation from each other. The complete and comprehensive science education program designed by teachers to meet the needs of the students should also demonstrate effective and meaningful performance-based assessment practices.

As the curriculum and overall set of experiences for students become better codified, so must the various formal and informal support systems for teachers and students. In addition, the expectations that the community and other teachers hold for each other likewise need to be reconsidered so as to be consistent with the inquiry-driven practices that the NSES support.

PROGRAM STANDARD A

All elements of the K–12 science program must be consistent with the other National Science Education Standards and with one another and developed within and across grade levels to meet a clearly stated set of goals.

- In an effective science program, a set of clear goals and expectations for students must be used to guide the design, implementation, and assessment of all elements of the science program.
- Curriculum frameworks should be used to guide the selection and development of units and courses of study.
- Teaching practices need to be consistent with the goals and curriculum frameworks.
- Assessment policies and practices should be aligned with the goals, student expectations, and curriculum frameworks.
- Support systems and formal and informal expectations of teachers must be aligned with the goals, student expectations, and curriculum frameworks.
- Responsibility needs to be clearly defined for determining, supporting, maintaining, and upgrading all elements of the science program.

Try This! 5–1 *Curriculum Analysis—Implementation*

SUPPORTING SCIENCE PROGRAM STANDARD A

Interview your instructor for this course: What decisions did your instructor make regarding textbook selection for this course? Is there a set of standards your instructor is trying to address? What is the relationship between this course and other courses in your program? What sort of activities did your instructor select and why? Your instructor's answers to those questions are factors that you will need to take into consideration as you develop science experiences for your students.

 ## Try This! 5–2 *Curriculum Analysis*

SUPPORTING SCIENCE PROGRAM STANDARD A

Obtain a curriculum document from a local school district (most are available online) and compare the science curriculum for the grade or subject you anticipate teaching with either the content standards from the National Science Education Standards, the scope and sequence statements from Benchmarks for Scientific Literacy, or your own state's science learning standards. How did one of the above documents influence the development and content of local learning standards? If the local district has a science coordinator or a curriculum coordinator, it might be instructive to interview this person to see how they see the alignment of the various sets of standards.

As a class assignment, brainstorm some essential questions regarding a set of standards and how they are operationalized in the district. Compare your findings with those of other students as they investigate the curriculum in other districts.

A final point of investigation: What does the district's curriculum look like in different classrooms? Is it clearly the same, or are practices different in different classrooms? Is this defensible, or is this desirable?

The final consideration for developing consistency between a school and a school district's science teaching practices is to develop long-term strategies for reflecting on and revising teaching and curriculum development practices. Meaningful change will not take place without identifying the need for change and accepting responsibility for serving as a leader to direct the change and growth in the program. As new materials and methods become available, they will not be implemented in any meaningful way unless there is a plan in place to identify, evaluate, and implement these elements into teaching practice.

Program Standard B

"Science for all Americans" is a theme that runs through much of the literature supporting science education. To accomplish this goal, it is clear that science education experiences must meet the needs of all of America's students and that

PROGRAM STANDARD B

The program of study in science for all students should be developmentally appropriate, interesting, and relevant to students' lives; emphasize student understanding through inquiry; and be connected with other school subjects.

- The program of study should include all of the content standards.
- Science content must be embedded in a variety of curriculum patterns that are developmentally appropriate, interesting, and relevant to students' lives.
- The program of study must emphasize student understanding through inquiry.
- The program of study in science should connect to other school subjects.

science experiences must help students understand both the content and problem-solving skills associated with learning science.

None of the content standards in the NSES, in *Benchmarks for Scientific Literacy*, or in any of the various state learning standards identify any one of the areas of science content as either more or less important than the others. The commitment to superior science teaching and learning experiences represented by the NSES assumes that science experiences will address all of the content standards. Whether the standards are achieved through problem-based learning or interdisciplinary instruction (or even traditional discipline-centered experiences) is not addressed; rather, the goal is that all students have a deep and meaningful relationship with the science content standards. An activity such as the one outlined in Try This! 5–3 offers an example of how interdisciplinary activities can provide more opportunities to teach science and, from the perspective of other disciplines, how other skills such as numeracy, language, and literacy may be developed within the context of science teaching. Approaches such as this should be highlighted during teacher preparation and supported by science education systems.

 Try This! 5–3 *Interdisciplinary Activities: Middle School Level**

SUPPORTING SCIENCE PROGRAM STANDARD B

Description of Activity

Students are given a ransom note and several black pens, each one belonging to a different suspect in the crime. Challenged to determine which of the black pens was used to write the ransom note, student-detectives explore the concepts of solubility, pigments, and separation of mixtures as they use chromatography to ferret out the culprit. Analyzing ink is one of many instances for which the technique of chromatography is used in science; the separation of blood and other constituents has become invaluable in real-world forensic science, and students' fascination with detective work makes a terrific springboard for further discussion. (Lawrence Hall of Science, 2005, paragraph 2.)

Reflection on these Activities

While a single set of interdisciplinary activities does not qualify as an entire science program or district curriculum, the curriculum should be flexible enough to support these practices.

The interdisciplinary potential of an experience like this is clear: the chance to read and write mysteries, to see how forensic science is used in detective work, and to see how evidence is used in both a scientific and a civic sense.

*Adapted and modified from the Great Explorations in Math and Science (GEMS) teacher's guide entitled Crime Lab Chemistry *(Barber, 1985). Copyright by The Regents of the University of California.*

The final elements of Standard B focus on the connection between the study of science and students' lives, other school subjects, and an emphasis on an inquiry-based approach for students' learning.

 ## Try This! 5–4   *What Is Inquiry?*

SUPPORTING SCIENCE PROGRAM STANDARD B

During a field placement this semester, interview your mentor/cooperating teacher about what it looks like when they teach science through inquiry. Find out how they define inquiry. How often do they use inquiry as opposed to other methods as they teach science? What influences their decisions? Compare your findings with your classmates during a follow-up class session. As you summarize the class's findings, what common themes do you see as you look at how inquiry is defined and used? What differences arise? How is your teacher's understanding similar or different from yours and your classmates?

The science we wish children to experience must be designed in such a way as to present engaging and developmentally appropriate experiences to children. The instructional danger of presenting highly abstract information, such as understanding molecules or a conceptual understanding of density, should be prevented by reserving such content for at least the upper elementary grades.

In addition to ensuring that the content is developmentally appropriate, seeking to promote the relevancy of science to the lives of students is also important. Sometimes this is accomplished by attending to students' curiosity about the world around them, but more fundamentally, examining issues related to their lives, such as biodiversity, pollution, ecology, and the impact of technology on their lives, offers an excellent means for promoting a connection between the academic world and the nonacademic world.

Supporting these experiences, the goal of having students learn science through inquiry remains the core of the National Science Education Standards. While individual teachers working in individual classrooms have always shown the commitment to teaching science through inquiry, it has not necessarily been institutionally supported through the entire curriculum or school district science programs. King, Shumow, and Lietz (2001) recount a case study examination of teachers in a large school district that revealed a lack of genuine inquiry in the experiences the teachers delivered to their students, and they had difficulty even defining what inquiry *is*. The purpose here is not to criticize teachers, but to recognize that they require support through their teacher preparation coursework, through staff development, and through reconceptualizing the science program in a way that embraces inquiry-rich practices.

"The program of study in science should connect to other school subjects" (National Academy of Sciences, 1996, p. 212). The focus on interdisciplinary instruction has long been a strong theme within the elementary school and in middle schools that embrace the conceptual tenants of middle school education. Formalized connections at the secondary level are far less common. But, as the opportunities arise, their school experiences should be as interdisciplinary in nature as is reasonable, which presents obvious challenges when teachers are prepared at the secondary level as content area specialists. Having a program that allows teachers the flexibility to have students investigate real-world problems (which are necessarily interdisciplinary) as a means of addressing science content is an excellent first step.

Program Standard C

As stated in Program Standard C, having the science curriculum reflect more of an interdisciplinary perspective is desirable. The National Council of Teachers of Mathematics (NCTM (1991)) note in their Standard 4: Mathematical Concepts, Procedures, and Connections states that teachers should emphasize "connections between mathematics and other disciplines and connections to daily living" (p. 89). The *NCTM Standards for Curriculum and Evaluation* (NCTM, 1989) also seeks to develop connections between and among mathematics and other disciplines with the standard explicitly stating that students "use mathematics in other curriculum areas" (p. 32). Besides using mathematics as part of science instruction, other uses of mathematics, such as modeling concepts through equations, can provide an important strategy for integrating science and mathematics.

> **PROGRAM STANDARD C**
>
> The science program should be coordinated with the mathematics program to enhance student use and understanding of mathematics in the study of science and to improve student understanding of mathematics.

 Try This! 5–5 *Sample Activity: The Big Banana Peel**

SUPPORTING SCIENCE PROGRAM STANDARD C

Key Question

How much of a banana is edible?

Background Information

This may be the students' first experience in writing a formula. If so, the development of a formula needs to be discussed. In this case, the edible portion of a banana (E in the formula) is to be expressed as a fraction or percentage of the total mass of the banana (T in the formula). Thus, if one-half of the banana is edible, the formula would be $E = 1/2T$. Most bananas will come very close to the formula $E = .65T$ or $E = 2/3T$.

Students may reason that the coefficient of T must be less than one since the edible portion has a mass less than the total. The best way to determine a formula for a group of bananas is by an average percentage. The function of an average is to help guard against significant error. In this case, the average will be in the neighborhood of 65 percent, depending on the ripeness of the banana. Percentages are not normally used in such formulas, so 65 percent is not an appropriate form. It should be converted to a decimal such as .65. The formula becomes $E = .65T$.

Fact pages can be included to provide information about the science of the banana plant, the nature of bananas as a food product, the origin of bananas, and sources of bananas as an agricultural commodity.

Procedure

1. Begin by administering the following four-point true-false quiz to heighten interest and peak curiosity. Students may indicate their responses by showing thumbs up for "I think this is a true statement" and thumbs down for "I think this is a false statement." (No sideways thumbs!) The four statements are these:

   a. The banana is a berry. (true)

   b. Bananas grow on trees. (false)

   c. Pound for pound, bananas are the most widely sold fruit in the United States. (true)

   d. Bananas are highly nutritious and easily digestible. (true)

2. Distribute a banana to each group. Direct them to complete and record the masses of the whole banana, the edible part, and the peel. It is important to make three different measures rather than two in which case the mass of the peeling would be subtracted from the total to obtain the mass of the edible portion. By completing three measurements, students have more experience using the balances and more opportunities to check their accuracy. (Note that the sum of the masses in the second and third columns should approximate the mass in the first. Approximate? Yes! Measurement is always approximate, and the sum may differ by just one gram from the mass in the first column since students are measuring to the nearest gram and therefore rounding. Students therefore have a realistic experience with the fact that measurement is approximate.)

3. Have each group share their data for the first three columns of the table. Direct all groups to make the computations to finish the table.

4. After the averages have been computed and recorded, encourage students to construct the bar graphs.

5. Students are asked to write a formula relating the mass of the edible portion (E) to the total mass of the banana (T).

Discussion

1. What percentage of a banana is edible?

2. What factors might affect this result? How? (ripeness, size, variety)

3. If bananas are priced at 49 cents per pound, how much money is wasted on the skin that is thrown away?

4. What other fruits have an inedible peeling. Which fruits have a higher percentage of edible mass?

Extensions

1. Try bananas of different sizes and stages of ripeness.

2. See how plantains compare with bananas.

Reflection on Activity

This activity allows students to use mathematical modeling to describe a banana. While there are obviously many important characteristics to consider when defining a banana, using mathematics to describe quantitatively a property of a banana has the potential of giving students insights into a substance that would not be easily achieved any other way.

    This activity also allows experience, knowledge, and skills from both mathematics and science to fuse seamlessly.

*From the activity The Big Banana Peel. Published by the AIMS Education Foundation (www.aimsedu.org). Used by permission.

Activities such as "The Big Banana Peel" (see Try This! 5–5) provide one example of how concepts in mathematics and science can be developed and exploited in tandem. While it is evident that many teachers will conduct math and science interdisciplinary experiences as part of their instructional practices, it is desirable to orchestrate and coordinate these integrated experiences so that they happen more consistently and result from coherent planning rather than serendipity.

As with other parts of the curriculum, it is sometimes easier to develop integrated math and science experiences at the elementary and middle school level. For those who seek a more transparent connection between the disciplines, experiences of teachers such as Sean O'Connor (2003) offer hope as he describes his successes in making the content of his high school chemistry course a means of developing algebra skills. Understanding the nature of both disciplines and using the process skills associated with both disciplines offers one strategy for seamless delivery of instruction in both disciplines (Roebuck & Warden, 1998). Similar opportunities exist for thoughtful teachers in biology, physics, astronomy, and physical science as well.

The challenges of integrating math and science instruction—time, coordination, current lack of instructional models, and system-wide achievement expectations (Huntley, 1998)—are real. The potential student outcomes—understanding the relationship between math and science, enhanced problem-solving skills, an appreciation for real-world connections between the academic world and the nonacademic world, and the promise of high achievement for all students—make it a challenge worth taking.

Program Standard D

The elements of Program Standard D have been part of science education discussions for decades. The National Society for the Study of Education concluded their 1960 yearbook on the improvement of science education with a number of questions. Among them: How can an adequate supply of competent science teachers be maintained? How can the adequacy of facilities for instruction in science be increased? How can the time available for teaching science be most equitably allocated? Clearly, the development of science education programs and effective delivery continue to be issues that consume many of those who think deeply about science experiences for children. It is clear as well that those questions are present in Program Standard D.

Of all the requirements for a successful science program, the key resource is the teachers. Simply in terms of the financial investment of a school district, teacher salaries are the largest single outlay of expenses for a school district.

> **PROGRAM STANDARD D**
>
> The K–12 science program must give students access to appropriate and sufficient resources, including quality teachers, time, materials and equipment, adequate and safe space, and the community.
>
> - The most important resource is professional teachers.
> - Time is a major resource in a science program.
> - Conducting scientific inquiry requires that students have easy, equitable, and frequent opportunities to use a wide range of equipment, materials, supplies, and other resources for experimentation and direct investigation of phenomena.
> - Collaborative inquiry requires adequate and safe space.
> - Good science programs require access to the world beyond the classroom.

Nationally, over 85 percent of the $410.6 billion spent on education went to support instruction; $210 billion of those funds were directed to teachers' salaries (U.S. Census Bureau, 2003). The dollars committed to teachers underscore their key role in the process. Attention to teachers is also a highlight of the federal government's No Child Left Behind legislation, with its goal of producing "highly qualified" teachers, is particularly difficult to meet this demand in rural and urban areas. While the government is allowing greater flexibility in how to demonstrate this competence (U.S. Department of Education, 2003), the emphasis on highly trained and competent teachers is a centerpiece of the legislation.

"Time is a major resource in a science program" (National Academy of Sciences, 1996, p. 218), and as all practicing teachers are aware, it is a commodity that is consistently in short supply. While teachers at the middle and secondary level have the luxury of specific time set aside during the day for delivering science content, issues related to academic testing have started to draw time away from the delivery of academic experiences. For elementary teachers, the time pressure to teach science (and other disciplines, such as social studies, art, music, and so on) faces greater jeopardy. The recognition that science is an important content area must come not only from the teachers and the community, but also from people who design and implement science programs. Worthy goals lead to frustration if there is neither time nor other resources available to implement the program.

Access to appropriate material to engage in scientific inquiry immediately follows the presence of a skilled and empathetic teacher in importance. Regarding Mr. McKee's experiences at the beginning of the chapter, one of his other programmatic awakenings during his time on the school district's curriculum council related to funding for science materials for K–6 students in his local district. A curriculum council recommendation was made to continue funding for science materials at fifty cents per child—per year. When he expressed some concern that this might not be adequate, he was informed that the previous level of funding was set at twenty-five cents per child per year—so the fifty-cent level was regarded as a substantial improvement!

Hopefully, budgets are not so parsimonious in the schools and school districts where you will be teaching. While time is tight and scarce dollars are allocated toward salaries, administration, and the physical plant, access to materials is essential. Through recent federal legislation, modest tax breaks are being offered to teachers in recognition of their very real contributions to their classrooms by purchasing their own materials, but not all teachers can afford to supplement their school's material budget—nor should they ethically be expected to. School boards and other funding agencies need to recognize that exemplary teaching requires access to appropriate material's which require adequate resources.

As effective inquiry-enriched teaching takes place, it is worth remembering that the safety of students is a fundamental concern for all educators (American Chemical Society, 2001). In addition to safe space, sufficient space for groups of students to work together is essential, as is safe storage for materials that are used over extended periods of time. Some teachers meet this need through unorthodox means, such as hanging student-constructed kites from the ceiling to store them prior to flying (King, 2004). Hopefully, counter space and cupboard space are not such premium commodities in the schools in which you will be teaching.

Access to information beyond the classroom is also needed to support inquiry-based practices. Various technologies have been touted as helping students and teachers breach the walls of the classroom, whether it is the motion picture, radio, television, or, most recently, the computer (King, 2001a; 2001b).

Improvements in technology allow computers to provide a dialogic interaction between the school and the outside world. While television, movies, and the radio bring information to the students from external sources, the information has been selected by the teacher in advance because it meets a particular need. The dialog possible through telecommunications allows a discussion to take place between students and experts in many fields.

The challenge is to ensure that students have access to this rich source of information. While the safety of the student is paramount, it is important to ensure that there is telecommunications access to the world beyond the classroom—likely through a teacher's school district email system.

Recall Mr. Dreyer's experience described in Chapter 2. He had to advocate for his students to gain access to a telephone within the school as they contacted and collaborated with outside consultants and experts in their problem-based learning experiences. Mr. Dreyer recounted that in all of the internal obstacles he had to deal with to implement his curriculum of real-world problem-solving, access to the telephones was second in difficulty to getting his students access to a copy machine.

Program Standard E

The issue was clearly articulated by the North Central Regional Educational Laboratory (NCREL):

> **PROGRAM STANDARD E**
>
> All students in the K–12 science program must have equitable access to opportunities to achieve the National Science Education Standards.

All students deserve equitable access to challenging and meaningful learning and achievement in science, regardless of race, ethnic group, gender, socioeconomic status, geographic location, age, language, disability, or prior science achievement. This concept has profound implications for teaching and learning science throughout the school community. It suggests that ensuring equity and excellence must be at the core of systemic reform efforts, not only in science, but in education as a whole.

Educators and community members are becoming increasingly aware that most students, particularly ethnic and language minorities and females, are not being served adequately by many existing science programs. Traditional patterns of science education have contributed to widespread scientific illiteracy among students and adults and a serious under representation of minorities and females in scientific and technical careers. (NCREL, 1995, paragraphs 1–2)

Program Standard E has a strong political subtext associated with it. As stated above, there is consensus that all students, regardless of gender, national origin, social status, or any other factor should be held to high standards. To that end, school programs and teacher preparation should support students in attaining these high standards.

There are a variety of resources in place to encourage underrepresented groups to participate in science. Grant-funded programs, teacher workshops, summer institutes for teachers and students, and other initiatives seek to promote scientific learning and careers in science. Methods courses advocate strategies that may be used as preservice teachers work toward the goal of all students having success in science. A quick search of the U.S. Department of Education web site yielded in excess of 500 grants to support teachers of all grade levels in a multitude of content areas. An instructive exercise for any reader who wants to improve instruction and gather additional resources might well start with a visit to the search function at http://www.ed.gov/ index.jhtml.

Equity issues have profound consequences for education in general, and the ideal of achieving equity is exceedingly difficult to accomplish. In many communities, the challenges of limited resources prevent meeting the equity needs of students.

Arguments concerning funding are frustrating and politically charged. Jonathan Kozol (1967; 1991; 1995) has written at length for the last four decades about the challenges associated with inequities in society, the plight of children, and the devastating effects that underfunding education has on children in under-resourced schools. In the early years of the twenty-first century, in uncertain economic times, the challenges are even greater and the need for equity in education is greater still.

Program Standard F

While teaching science so that all children enjoy opportunities for success is a challenge, a cynic might suggest that getting teachers and administrators to work together provides even greater challenges. Both groups have similar goals and both groups see the same issues that can make science teaching such a trial. Perceptive leadership—from teachers and from administrators—needs to help both parties see that their respective views on the tasks of teaching science are complementary and support each other. The reform efforts that the National Science Education Standards promote may best be accomplished in an environment that encourages and supports trust and openness and encourages collegiality among the teachers themselves and between teachers and administrators.

> **PROGRAM STANDARD F**
>
> Schools must work as communities that encourage, support, and sustain teachers as they implement an effective science program.
>
> - Schools must explicitly support reform efforts in an atmosphere of openness and trust that encourages collegiality.
> - Regular time needs to be provided and teachers encouraged to discuss, reflect, and conduct research around science education reform.
> - Teachers must be supported in creating and being members of networks of reform.
> - An effective leadership structure that includes teachers must be in place.

The program development standards identified in Standard F are factors that need to be present for school district staff members to support program changes that support interdisciplinary and integrated teaching and a commitment to teaching science as inquiry.

"Regular time needs to be provided and teachers encouraged to discuss, reflect, and conduct research around science education reform" (National Academy of Sciences, 1996, p. 222). While this *sounds* straightforward, time is a precious commodity in the classroom. Administrators can support this by allowing time for sufficient planning and reflecting as the school schedule is developed. Teachers need to develop a broader definition of what "planning time" connotes. To support the reflective process, it needs to move from simply reflections on anecdotal experiences, which are profoundly important, to more data-driven experiences (Dana & Yendol-Silva, 2003). Four definitions of action research offer this perspective:

- Action Research is a three-step spiral process of (1) planning which involves reconnaissance; (2) taking actions; and (3) fact-finding about the results of the action. (Attributed to Kurt Lewin, 1947)

- Action Research is the process by which practitioners attempt to study their problems scientifically in order to guide, correct, and evaluate their decisions and actions. (Attributed to Stephen Corey, 1953)

- Action Research in education is study conducted by colleagues in a school setting of the results of their activities to improve instruction. (Attributed to Carl Glickman, 1992)

- Action Research is a fancy way of saying let's study what's happening at our school and decide how to make it a better place. (Attributed to Emily Calhoun, 1994) (Miller, no date, paragraphs 1–4)

The common element to these definitions is the use of school and classroom-derived data to make instructional changes. As preservice teachers, your clinical supervisor will collect data on your progress during your clinical and student teaching experiences. This data is used to help you become a more effective teacher. The difference between "nice job" and "my checklist shows that you only called on four students in the class—all boys" is not just the difference between the general and the specific, but it allows you to identify an existing situation, compare it to the goal, and formulate action to achieve that goal. Action research is an excellent tool to use for instructional, curricular, and programmatic improvement. Sagor (2000) offers additional suggestions as to how to do

✓ Try This! 5–6 *Instructional Change*

SUPPORTING SCIENCE PROGRAM STANDARD F

Interview a teacher. How do they plan for instructional changes? What sort of formative data do they collect? How do they know when a change is needed and how do they go about implementing instructional change?

If your teacher has had some experience applying an action research model to his or her professional practice, ask them to share what they have done, what they learned, and how they made instructional adjustments, based on what they learned during their investigation.

effective action research in classrooms and schools, with a focus on how to use it to meet the specific needs of the classroom or school district.

Change will not take place if teachers are working in isolation. Among the key elements leading to instructional change, (Fullan, 1993), two are especially appropriate to our current discussion: "Connection with the wider environment is critical for success" (p. 129) and "Every person is a change agent" (p. 130). These two points taken together underscore the value of each individual to the success of desired instructional changes. Besides the value and importance of the individual, it is essential that teachers be genuine functioning parts of a system, and they must be supported in their role as members of this system.

No educational reform will be functional if it has not taken teachers into consideration. To ensure that change is effective, a supportive and effective organization with a sound leadership structure must be in place.

Implications for Practice

There are a number of issues to consider as you consider what a science education program looks like. There will already be a science education program with an attendant curriculum in place when you arrive in your clinical and student teaching sites and in the school and district where you begin your teaching career. While your time as a teacher–student is not the time to begin action in curriculum development, this is an appropriate time to learn what the big issues are and to see how those issues are implemented in the schools where you will be teaching. As with action research, knowing your desired goal and collecting data during your teaching experiences also applies to the bigger and possibly more challenging goal of changing programs and curriculum on a larger scale.

CLASSROOM SNAPSHOTS

NSES-Informed Science Program

Two years later, Mike was a more satisfied member of both his community and the school district's curriculum council. After his initial surprise about the way the school district's science program was organized, he made the decision that he would not run away; he would commit three years to the committee and see what he could accomplish in that amount of time.

Two things helped him make progress. One was a bit of luck—the other was intentional. The lucky part was the arrival of a new curriculum director for the school district, Dr. Jill Bird. She had a perspective similar to Mike's about what constituted good science instruction and saw herself in the district for a long period of time—long enough to effect some degree of institutional change.

The intentional part was his decision to work actively with the teachers on the committee as an advocate. The lucky part was Mike's current job was a consultant, as he had time available during the day to work as an advocate for the teachers and the administrative staff as well.

Building a team, having consistent goals, and appreciating the long-term challenges ahead were all parts of the process. While only two years had elapsed since his original encounter with the curriculum process in his school district, Mike, Jill, and their colleagues could see both progress and more challenges ahead.

Planning and understanding the nature of change were essential elements of the change process in this setting. While tenacity and serendipity both played a role in the process, the likelihood of success was enhanced by effective planning. Following a curriculum described by Glatthorn (1994), Mike and Jill worked hard to lay the groundwork to support change by identifying the current state of the district's curriculum and making plans for long-term change. The process moved steadily as teachers in the district (similar to the teachers who will be described in Chapter 6 on professional development standards) were eager to move beyond current practices and into practices aligned with an inquiry focus. Through the efforts of these three parties—administrators, community members, and the teachers—the vision of an inquiry-based curriculum moved away from happenstance without coordination. Instead, it became a model of instruction for all teachers within the district.

No, not all teachers accepted the change, but because a coherent plan had been developed and there was significant buy-in from all constituencies, the envisioned changes in the curriculum had the promise of success rather than the expectation of continued mediocrity.

Summary

As with the other vignettes profiled in this book, Mike's experience as a community member of the curriculum council is not a work of fiction. He is an acquaintance of mine who had this experience. His commitment to a National Science Education Standards-informed vision of teaching in his local school district is certainly commendable. Perhaps more so was his desire to not simply give up in the face of what initially was perceived as overwhelming institutional barriers. Building a small community of like-minded agents of change who have at their disposal a really good idea—such as the NSES—is the first step toward profound institutional change.

References

Abruscato, J. (2000). *Teaching children science (5th edition)*. Boston: Allyn & Bacon.

AIMS Education Foundation. (1987). The big banana peel. *Math and science: A solution*. Fresno, CA: AIMS Educational Foundation.

Alberts, B. M. & Heyman, I. M. (1997). *Science for all children*. Washington, DC: National Science Resource Center.

American Chemical Society. (2001). *Chemical safety for teachers and their supervisors*. Retrieved on April 20, 2004, from http://membership.acs.org/c/ccs/pubs/chemical_safety_manual.pdf

Barber, J. (1985). *Crime lab chemistry*. Berkeley, CA: Lawrence Hall of Science.

Carin, A. A. & Bass, J. E. (2001). *Methods of teaching science as inquiry. (8th edition)*. Upper Saddle River, NJ: Merrill.

Dana, N. F. & Yendol-Silva, D. (2003). *The reflective educator's guide to classroom research.* Thousand Oaks, CA: Corwin Press.

Etheredge, S. & Rudnitsky, A. (2003). *Introducing students to scientific* inquiry. Boston: Allyn & Bacon.

Fullan, M. G. (1991). *The new meaning of educational change.* New York: Teachers College.

Fullan, M. G. (1993). Innovation, reform, and restructuring strategies. In G. Cawelti (Ed), *Challenges and achievements of American Education* (pp 116–133). Alexandria, VA: Association for Supervision and Curriculum Development.

Glatthorn, A. A. (1994). *Developing a quality curriculum.* Alexandria, VA: Association for Supervision and Curriculum Development.

Huntley, M. A. (1998). Design and implementation of a framework for defining integrated mathematics and science education. *School Science and Mathematics, 98*(6), 320–327.

King, K. P. (2001a). *Technology, science teaching and literacy: A century of growth.* New York: Kluwer.

King, K. P. (2001b). Automation, innovation, participation: Infusing technology into the social studies. In P. J. Farris, *Elementary and middle school social studies: An integrated approach* (pp. 350–372). Boston: McGraw-Hill.

King, K. P. (2004, March). Ever fly a tetrahedron? *Science Scope, 26*(6), 25–29.

King, K., Shumow, L., & Lietz, S. (2001). Science education in an urban elementary school: Case studies of teacher beliefs and classroom practices. *Science Education, 85*(2), 89–110.

Kozol, J. (1967). *Death at an early age.* Boston: Houghton Mifflin.

Kozol, J. (1991). *Savage inequalities.* New York: HarperPerennial.

Kozol, J. (1995). *Amazing grace.* New York: HarperPerennial.

Krajcik, J., Czerniak, C. & Berger, C. (1999). *Teaching children science: A project-based approach.* Boston: McGraw-Hill.

Lawrence Hall of Science. (2005). LHS GEMS, Crime Lab Chemistry. Retrieved on June 2, 2006 from http://www.lawrence hall of science/gems/GEM170.html

Lawrence Hall of Science. (2003). LHS GEMS, Crime Lab Chemistry. Berkeley, CA: Lawrence Hall of Science. Retrieved on April 25, 2004, from http://www.lhsgems.org/GEM170.html

Massell, D. (1994). Achieving consensus: Setting the agenda for state curriculum reform. In *Governance of curriculum* (pp. 84–108). Alexandria, VA: ASCD.

Miller, C. A. (no date). Action research as a framework for school improvement. Boca Raton, FL: Florida Atlantic University. Retrieved on April 23, 2004, from http://www.coe.fau.edu/sfcel/define.htm

National Council of Teachers of Mathematics. (1989). *NCTM standards for curriculum and evaluation.* Reston, VA: National Council of Teachers of Mathematics.

National Council of Teachers of Mathematics. (1991). *NCTM professional teaching standards/evaluation.* Reston, VA: National Council of Teachers of Mathematics.

National Research Council. (1996). *National science education standards.* National Academy Press: Washington, DC.

National Society for the Study of Education. (1960). *Fifty-ninth yearbook: Rethinking science education.* Chicago: University of Chicago Press.

North Central Regional Educational Laboratory. (1995). Critical issue: Ensuring equity and excellence in science. Oak Brook, IL: North Central Regional Educational Laboratory. Retrieved on April 22, 2004, from http://www.ncrel.org/sdrs/areas/issues/content/cntareas/science/sc200.htm

O'Connor, S. (2003). Connecting algebra and chemistry. *The Science Teacher, 70*(1), 38–40.

Roebuck, K. I. & Warden, M. A. (1998). Searching for the center on the math-science continuum. *School Science and Mathematics, 98*(6), 328–333.

Sagor, R. (2000). *Guiding school improvement with a action research.* Alexandria, VA: ASCD.

United States Census Bureau. (2003). *Public education finances 2001.* Washington, DC: U.S. Census Bureau. Retrieved on April 19, 2004, from http://ftp2.census.gov/govs/school/01fullreport.pdf

United States Department of Education. (2004). New *No Child Left Behind* Flexibility: Highly Qualified Teachers. Washington, DC: U.S. Department of Education. Retrieved on April 19, 2004, from http://www.ed.gov/nclb/methods/teachers/hqtflexibility.pdf

CHAPTER 6

Standards For Science Education Systems

CLASSROOM SNAPSHOTS

Late one April morning, Matt Kelly glanced out the window of his Biological Evolution class and saw a pair of finches fly by the window and then alight on a bird feeder full of thistle feed. The discussions in class had briefly mentioned the presence of finches on the Galapagos Islands, which catalyzed Darwin's thinking about evolution. That intriguing but very brief discussion about how Darwin used his experiences to recognize evolution as a means of explaining change among species over time had profoundly captured Matt's imagination. The variety of beaks on Darwin's finches was amazing, and as Matt watched the finches on the feeder outside his classroom, he smiled with personal satisfaction at the knowledge of how those finchs' beaks were suited exactly right for consuming the thistle seed in the feeder.

Unfortunately, his time since then had consisted only of calculating probabilities of various alleles being passed on from one generation to another. Looking back at the chalkboard, he finished copying the professor's formula into his own notebook ". . . linkage disequilibrium (D) is calculated as $D = f(A1B1) * f(A2B2) - f(A1B2) * f(A2B1)$ (where $f(X)$ is the frequency of X in the population) . . ." (Origins Archive, 1996). True, it was interesting stuff as well, but as he looked outside at the finches again and thought about how he might be teaching this same content to his students some day . . . but the question still nagging him was *how*?

Walking back to his apartment after class, Matt saw the finches again. As he thought about the role of that type of bird in the history of biology and understanding evolution, he began to wonder how his previous biology course had prepared him to take his current evolution class. Thoughts blurred . . . and coalesced: "vocabulary . . . of course. An overview of evolution . . . yes, that had given me a broader point of view that helped make the evolution class make more sense. More important . . . understanding relationships among concepts." Matt didn't normally see himself as overly reflective, but there were some ideas about teaching and learning that were coming into focus as he walked across campus. Indeed, he wondered, "What is this course preparing me to do?"

Clearly, as a biology major, his instructor had made it evident that the materials covered during the course would be important for other coursework in biology. This was valuable, he reflected, as each course needed to reinforce others to create a coherent program. The larger question that he now posed to himself: "Is this all coursework is supposed to do—prepare me to take the next class?" was not a question he was prepared to answer, at least at this point in his program of study.

Related to the questions he had been asking himself regarding what his current course was preparing him to do, Matt's mind wandered to how his previous courses had prepared him for the bio course—and what else? He had known from the start that he wanted to teach biology after he graduated from State. As he watched his professors and graduate assistants, he not only thought about what they were teaching him, but how they stacked up as potential role models for him as a teacher. What was it in the process or the content of the teaching he had been exposed to that was going to help him become a teacher, and how were his courses doing more than simply preparing him for the next course in the sequence?

But for his career plans, one question still remained: How did these courses help him understand how to teach science to middle and high school students? If he wanted to imitate one of his less inspired teachers from high school, all it would take is simply using his class notes from his introductory college biology class and parroting them back to his future students. But Ms. Sabiduría, another one of his high school teachers, seemed to have a knack for explaining even difficult concepts to students in a way that made them seem obvious. Where did that ability come from? What did she know about her discipline that helped her use her knowledge to teach it so well? Or maybe she was just a "natural teacher," if there was such a thing.

As he mounted the steps to his apartment, Matt's thoughts were still raging. Perhaps after lunch—and a nap—things might seem clearer.

Introduction

Matt's reflections are issues that many of you have to come to terms with. For students who major in elementary education, the challenge can be greater still, as the coursework that many of you took to meet your science requirements for your elementary education degree was very likely three introductory-level science courses: perhaps introductory biology, introductory geology, and basic chemistry. These are imminently worthy courses. The challenge faced by those of us who wish to make a career of teaching—whether it be a secondary science major who wishes to teach a science discipline at a high school or an elementary teacher who will teach science as one of a number of content areas, is how to connect what we learn in our science coursework with what we must know about the discipline to teach children effectively.

It is hoped that those who major in a content area will, by virtue of taking extensive coursework in that area, be able to build the broad conceptual understanding necessary to teach science to their students. The problem that Matt reflected on during his walk across campus is essentially a matter of how he knows what he knows and how he can translate that to teaching knowledge.

As we examine the Standards profiled in this chapter, our goal is to see how science education systems—teacher preparation, student learning, and teachers teaching other teachers—may be better coordinated with each other. How better coordination of resources and experiences can contribute to more successful science experiences—and making better use of limited resources for program development—will form the core discussion for this chapter.

Changing Emphases

In previous chapters, it was possible to identify a series of recommended changes in practice for each of the Standards. The changing standards for science education systems are slightly different in this chapter than in the previous chapters: we have to examine changes at the federal, state, and local levels. While some of the experiences parallel each other, there are specific issues related to each level of science education systems that we need to address.

It is also hoped that these desired changes in science education systems will be seen as a means of institutionalizing the practices discussed in previous chapters. The case made for effective and meaningful professional development programs in Chapter 5 remains important, but there is a larger goal of coordinating these changes across local, state, and federal domains.

Over the decades, support has been given for the development of science curriculum by the National Science Foundation (NSF) and other agencies. The increase in NSF funding from 1953 ($10,000) to 1959 ($40,000,000) to support science teaching and science curriculum development (Carin, Bass, & Contant, 2005) resulted in a plethora of science curriculum: SCIS, SAPA, ESS, PSSC, CBA, ESCP, FOSS, GEMS, and a variety of others. Many of the early programs broke new ground for science curricula and applied learning theory to science curriculum. Others modeled the process of performing science as scientists do; still others sought to integrate instruction across the disciplines.

Presently, the need for curriculum support remains, but now the goal is to support curriculum development within the goals of the National Science Education Standards. Working to ensure that content, methods of inquiry, and performance-based assessment are all integral parts of the curriculum should be evident as new curricula are developed and disseminated.

Professional activities are part of a teacher's job, but are unobserved by the general public. Indeed, the young child playing teacher, laying the foundation for a future role in education, captures some of the classroom experience, but the professional experiences that take place beyond the classroom are not known by the child.

The text in Table 6.1 clarifies the nature of the changes in support between local school systems and the federal government. Many professional growth

TABLE 6.1 Changing Emphases for Science System Standards—Federal System*

Less Emphasis On	More Emphasis On
Financial support for developing new curriculum materials not aligned with the Standards	Financial support for developing new curriculum materials aligned with the Standards
Support by federal agencies for professional development activities that affect only a few teachers	Support for professional activities that are aligned with the Standards and promote changes system-wide
Agencies working independently on various components of science education	Coordination among agencies responsible for science education
Support for activities and programs that are unrelated to Standards-based reform	Support for activities and programs that successfully implement the Standards at state and district levels
Federal efforts that are independent of state and local levels	Coordination of reform efforts at federal, state, and local levels
Short-term projects	Long-term commitment of resources to improving science education

*Reprinted with permission from *National Science Education Standards* © 1996 by the National Academy of Sciences, courtesy of the National Academies Press, Washington, DC, p. 239.

activities in the past have been designed to benefit small groups of teachers and, consequently, small groups of students. While this is clearly valuable, with limited resources being a "fact of life" for those of us in education in the early 2000s, it is reasonable to expect that the limited resources that remain available will be directed toward serving the largest number of teachers and will support changes in professional work and professional development consistent with the Standards across the entire system.

To accomplish this goal more effectively, the various agencies with an interest in supporting science teacher development need to coordinate their interests and their agendas to better prepare teachers to teach science through practices that support inquiry. Consistent with this vision, support for activities and programs that seek to support implementation of the Standards at district and state levels must be part of this coordinated effort.

These are part of the broad vision that needs to be in place to support effective changes in science teaching methodology. Broad visions—especially those as ambitious as changing the way that science is commonly taught in American schools—will require a long-term investment of both energy and resources. The observation that many of the challenges and goals for science education set down in *Rethinking Science Education* (National Society for the Study of Education, 1960) are as relevant today as they were in 1960 is a sobering reminder that change is difficult, challenging, and takes time. This was recognized as well by the American Association for the Advancement of Science's *Project 2061*: the name was selected with respect to the next time that Halley's comet will be visible to the naked eye, underscoring the long-term perspective that is needed in order to see changes take place in science education (AAAS, 2006, sidebar notation).

Standards set a desired goal for practice. The National Science Education Standards are in no way a proposal for a national curriculum or a prescription for how to "fix" the challenges science education faces. Instead, it seeks to offer goals that are consistent with practices, attitudes, and knowledge of how children best learn science and how teachers most effectively teach science. One of the first places to begin this process is to recognize the need to coordinate reform efforts through careful planning, using the goals implied by the NSES as the vision, and working together in education partnerships that cross many boundaries—federal, state, local—as well as educational and community groups. As Table 6.1 did for the federal level, Table 6.2 outlines changes taking place between states and local school systems.

TABLE 6.2 Changing Emphases for Science System Standards—State System*

Less Emphasis On	More Emphasis On
Independent initiatives to reform components of science education	Partnerships and coordination of reform efforts
Funds for workshops and programs having little connection to the Standards	Funds to improve curriculum and instruction based on the Standards
Frameworks, textbooks, and materials based on activities only marginally related to the Standards	Frameworks, textbooks, and materials adoption criteria aligned with national and state standards
Assessments aligned with the traditional content of science education	Assessments aligned with the Standards and the expanded view of science content
Current approaches to teacher education	University/college reform of teacher education to include science-specific pedagogy aligned with the Standards
Teacher certification based on formal, historically based requirements	Teacher certification that is based on understanding and abilities in science and science teaching

*Reprinted with permission from *National Science Education Standards* (©) 1966 by the National Academy of Sciences, courtesy of the National Academies Press, Washington, DC, pp. 239–240.

Implementing these changes requires resources. Change is neither cheap nor easy. Witness the evolution of the industry to help individuals and organizations manage and anticipate change, ranging from the whimsically cheesy to the clearly delineated. Beyond simply helping to manage changes in science education practices and systems, resources—real money—needs to be committed to cultivating and supporting desired changes in a manner that is consistent with the Standards.

Ensuring that textbooks and curriculum materials are a good "fit" with the Standards, along with school district and state education goals, is an ongoing process. Since the publication of the Standards in 1996, nearly all states have identified a set of science learning goals for their students. These state goals are consistent with the goals enumerated in the Standards. Progress also has been made in connecting the Standards with textbooks: indeed, this quality is now used as a marketing tool by a number of publishers (Decision Development Incorporated, 2000; Science Curriculum, Inc., no date). In regard to aligning textbooks with state standards, it may be noted that Texas and California have special state-only versions of textbooks produced for them by various publishers. This tacitly recognizes the clout afforded by their statewide textbook adoption process.

Movement toward performance-based assessments was addressed in detail in Chapter 3. The issues discussed in that chapter were designed to address assessment at the level of the classroom teacher. At the state level, with student assessments becoming more a part of school quality determinations, it becomes more important that assessment practices be developed and supported at the state level that reflect the type of science instruction that takes place in the schools. A performance-based approach will better encourage inquiry practices to become the norm in the schools.

The point that Matt was pondering in the opening vignette related to the need for science-specific pedagogy; that is, learning science in such a way as to be able to meaningfully communicate it to other people. It is implied throughout current practices at universities that exposure to abundant content will help the student understand their discipline in such a way as to naturally develop this professional knowledge. There is some debate about whether this takes place, as Sokolove's (1999) attempts to delevop inquiry-based experiences in large-group lecture settings testifies.

For elementary education majors, this problem is compounded by the observation that many do not earn a major in a discipline and earning it in a science discipline is almost unheard of. Helping these individuals develop appropriate science content and pedagogical understanding is a challenge, as taking three introductory courses in three different science fields does not, generally speaking, prepare them either as citizens to use their knowledge in support of an enlightened view of scientific literacy or even to teach the science content with a measure of expertise.

Some universities have noted this challenge and have implemented courses in science topics for elementary majors, with the deliberate plan of helping students understand the discipline in such a way as to be able to teach it effectively. It must be understood that these courses do not represent a "dumbing down" of the curriculum, but understanding it in a different way—a way that helps prospective teachers understand the content in order to teach it.

Preparation of teachers leads naturally into the certification of teachers. Teachers may be prepared to teach either through teacher certification programs, which are most common, or through means of alternative certification, which has grown in popularity in recent years. Regardless of the training, some credentialing process is in place in each state. Generally this process consists of the completion of coursework or a demonstration of equivalent skills from work or other training, supervised student teaching, and a demonstration of knowledge through testing. What this looks like in each state will vary; your instructor, advisor, or another local resource will help you organize experiences—or gain competencies—as you prepare for a career of teaching.

These practices have been in place, in one form or another, for decades. Current movements to ensure that teachers demonstrate high-level skills and to maintain their certification are seen through programs such as the National Board for Professional Teaching Standards (NBPTS) certification. The goal of this organization is to have participating teachers demonstrate their skills through various artifacts (student work, videotaped teaching episodes, knowledge of the content, and knowledge of how children learn) to ensure that they possess the skills associated with highly effective teachers (NBPTS, 2004). With the changes brought about by the *No Child Left Behind* (U.S. Department of Education, 2002) legislation, the goals of producing teachers characterized as highly qualified has taken on new meaning and new importance.

> The definition of "highly qualified" in the law requires that public elementary and secondary school teachers have obtained full state certification or passed the state teacher licensing examination; hold a license to teach in the state; and not have had a certificate or license requirement waived under emergency, temporary or provisional conditions. There are exceptions to this for certain teachers in charter schools or in alternate certification programs. (National Education Association, 2004, paragraph 2)

The full consequences and implementation of this law are still being debated as the deadline for implementation draws near. The goal of having highly prepared and exemplary teachers, however, remains on everyone's agenda.

As former Speaker of the House of Representatives Thomas P. "Tip" O'Neill acerbically remarked, "all politics are local." So it is with staff development. While an overarching concept of science education is essential, as is sufficient funding to implement the vision, nothing will get done unless action takes place at the local school level with real, practicing teachers. The evolution of local practices is summarized in Table 6.3.

Bartels (1999) echoed those same sentiments when he noted that American education's greatest asset—as well as its greatest liability—is its democratic

TABLE 6.3   Changing Emphases for Science System Standards—District System*

Less Emphasis On	More Emphasis On
Technical, short-term, in-service workshops	Ongoing professional development to support teachers
Policies unrelated to Standards-based reform	Policies designed to support changes called for in the Standards
Purchase of textbooks based on traditional topics	Purchase or adoption of curriculum aligned with the Standards and a conceptual approach to science teaching, including support for hands-on science materials
Standardized tests and assessments unrelated to Standards-based programs and practices	Assessments aligned with the Standards
Administration determining what will be involved in improving science education	Teacher leadership in improvement of science education
Authority at upper levels of educational system	Authority for decisions at level of implementation
School board ignorance of science education program	School board support of improvements aligned with the Standards
Local union contracts that ignore changes in curriculum, instruction, and assessment	Local union contracts that support improvements indicated by the Standards

*Reprinted with permission from *National Science Education Standards* © 1966 by the National Academy of Sciences, courtesy of the National Academies Press, Washington, DC, p. 240.

orientation. Changes in such an environment are slow, organic, and require considerable consensus before the change becomes widespread.

"Ongoing professional development to support teachers" (National Academy of Sciences, 1996, p. 240) needs to be contrasted with the short-term, spur-of-the-moment in-service experiences that some school districts substitute for meaningful and long-term staff development. Whereas giving a teacher a training session in using word processing or presentation software certainly meets a need among many teachers as we seek to incorporate technology into instruction, the resources invested in such one-shot staff development experiences would be better implemented in a long-range program of professional renewal.

The preferred long-range plan would be designed to encourage changes that are identified in the National Science Education Standards. Time frames from planning, implementing, and assessing the changes called for during the staff development process are of profound importance. Helping teachers teach through inquiry, helping teachers become more expert in content area knowledge—and even recognizing their own expertise as staff developers—are the changes that are called for in the Standards.

One of the opportunities to influence change in a school system is to develop or purchase curriculum that is consistent with the vision of the Standards. To this end, the curriculum should be characterized by hands-on/minds-on experiences and a genuine inquiry-based approach that is driven by student questions. This captures, in the words of Worth (1999), "the power of children's thinking" (p. 25). Support for the curriculum and the instructional approach that it advocates are expected; continued financial support to provide materials is likewise essential.

As discussed in the chapter on assessment, local efforts in revitalizing science instruction must include a commitment to and implementation of performance-based assessment practices. The challenge is to assess students in a meaningful way as they engage in doing science, rather than assessing how much information they have acquired.

Leadership by teachers to produce change is essential, as is giving teachers involved in developing and implementing these changes the authority to make these decisions. A serious discussion about whether teachers genuinely want this decision-making power—and whether administrators are genuinely willing to relinquish such power—will need to happen at the local level.

Two additional groups need to be players in this debate: teachers' unions and school boards. Flexibility in work roles and the administrative tasks to be assumed by teachers as leaders are not defined in most contracts by either the school board or by the teachers' bargaining unit. Allowing flexibility in teacher assignments is a challenge that should be embraced by teachers' unions; using this flexibility to "cut corners" in program delivery or as a cost savings can be a challenge for some boards to overcome. Both of these constituencies are in place, ultimately, to serve the needs of students, but finding common ground to implement effective science instruction is the challenge laid down here.

Examining and Interpreting the Science Education System Standards

The evolution of practices profiled above seeks to codify staff development practices that are long term and designed to support the use of the Standards. The evolution of practices also seeks to build better communication among the various parties who seek to improve science education at the policy level, at the administrative level, and at the practitioner level. Finally, creating a common vision of what science education should look like among all participants is the most critical change to embrace—for a common vision offers an opportunity for common practices to emerge.

System Standards A and B

There is a reason that neither the National Science Education Standards nor *Benchmarks for Scientific* Literacy have been described here—or anywhere else—as a national curriculum, because they are not.

It is well-recognized that a cultural value of American education is that of local control of education issues. The purpose of the Standards and other science education reform documents is not to produce the same curriculum or identical experiences for children across the country. Rather, while respecting local needs and local traditions, the goal of meeting local instructional needs through an instructional environment that supports hands-on inquiry remains firm.

SYSTEM STANDARD A

Policies that influence the practice of science education must be congruent with the program, teaching, professional development, assessment, and content standards while allowing for adaptation to local circumstances.

SYSTEM STANDARD B

Policies that influence science education should be coordinated within and across agencies, institutions, and organizations.

The changes that are desired involve the way that science curriculum is regarded (as an essential part of the K–16 experience, and not just something for a chosen few), how assessment should take place (in a manner that supports inquiry of students doing real science, not by memorizing factual knowledge), and the role of teachers in this process (as full partners who have professional knowledge and experiences to share, and not as mere technicians to implement the curriculum).

The goal of System Standard B is to create a system in which science education is coordinated across various levels of involvement.

✔ # Try This! 6–1 *Beyond the Classroom: Interacting with Scientists*

SUPPORTING SCIENCE EDUCATION SYSTEM STANDARD B

Opportunities for scientists to interact with students and teachers have been made possible with the advent of the Internet. In communities with national laboratories or universities and colleges with a research mission, direct involvement by scientists in the educational process can be implemented.

At Fermi National Accelerator Laboratory (2004), the Ask-a-Scientist program is well established:

Over the past years, Fermilab has hosted a Sunday afternoon program, inviting the public to visit the lab and meet with members of our scientific staff. [Recently the] Ask-a-Scientist evolved into a more formal once-a-month program in association with the Lederman Science Education Center staff. The program is usually held on the afternoon of the first Sunday of each month and lasts about two and a half hours. So far this year, Ask-a-Scientist has averaged approximately 105 visitors for each of the four Sunday afternoons.

Many of us find Ask-a-Scientist to be a very rewarding way to spend a Sunday afternoon," said Peter Garbincius, Fermilab physicist and one of the organizers of the Ask-a-Scientist program. "You get to meet the lab's neighbors and find out what they think about science and Fermilab. We have some scientists who regularly sign up for many of these programs every year." (paragraphs 3 and 4)

Coordination among local schools, school districts, state boards of education, colleges of education, and various governmental agencies needs to move beyond simply agreeing about science education and begin to function in a manner that shows they clearly share the same vision.

✔ **Try This! 6–2**   *Beyond the Classroom: Developing Content Knowledge*

SUPPORTING SCIENCE EDUCATION SYSTEM STANDARD B

Some opportunities exist for direct interactions between teachers, students, and scientists. The work sponsored by the Digital Library for Earth Science Education (2004), as one example, offers specific opportunities for scientists to work with teachers and students. The goals for this project are to help teachers and students improve their content knowledge, as well as to help students and teachers engage in inquiry-based practices as do professional scientists.

System Standard C

Instructional fads can be some of education's worst enemies. Open classrooms during the 1970s, the advent of high-stakes testing during the 1990s, programmed learning exercises from another era: these and other educational experiences, carried out spastically and frantically in order to raise test scores from one year to the next, give the impression of a badly controlled ship, lunging from port to port. While the need to embrace and plan for change is one of the themes underscoring this book, a related part of this message is that with a desire to engage in instructional change comes the need to carry out the change without shortcuts and compromises.

> **SYSTEM STANDARD C**
>
> Policies need to be sustained over sufficient time to provide the continuity necessary to bring about the changes required by the Standards.

Many of the instructional practices that end up being characterized as fads often become so because they are poorly implemented or overused as a panacea for all of education's problems. Cooperative grouping is one instructional strategy that, when well implemented, can offer an effective means of organizing instruction. When used to simply organize groups without identifying needs for individual accountability or it loses its effectiveness. Using it all of the time—rather than as one instructional strategy out of many—further undermines its effectiveness.

More recently, the use of multiple intelligences, which represents a reasonable means of addressing the instructional and learning strengths of a classroom, has been given instructional and theoretical weight beyond its original conception.

The policies that are implemented need to be sustained over a sufficient amount of time to make the changes meaningful and to make the changes felt deeply over time.

System Standard D

Only six words: "Policies must be supported with resources" (National Academy of Sciences, p. 232), but they are the most expensive words in the entire document. The message conveyed by System Standard D doesn't allow for any exceptions. Policy changes require an investment of sufficient resources, whether they be human, financial, or time.

> **SYSTEM STANDARD D**
>
> Policies must be supported with resources.

✓ Try This! 6–3   *Beyond the Classroom: Financing Science Education*

SUPPORTING SCIENCE EDUCATION SYSTEM STANDARD D

School budgets to support science teaching range from zero to several dollars per student. Select a science activity you have either taken part in as a student, taught as a student teacher or classroom teacher, or would like to teach. Find the cost to teach that lesson, based on the materials you would have to purchase. Find the average cost for this activity per student.

What are some ways you can bring the cost down? What are some ways that you can obtain funding to support the acquisition of materials?

Follow up these questions with a teacher interview. How much money do they get from their building budget to support science teaching? How much do they spend from their own pocket to support their teaching? How often do they make instructional decisions based on finances/resources as opposed to instructional effectiveness or need?

A debate has raged for decades regarding the cost of education. Many critics suggest that change can be accomplished for little or no cost, but only anecdotal evidence is offered to support the "no cost" case. These sorts of changes, however, tend not to be system-wide and more often than not cannot be transferred to another time or place. For change to be genuine and long-lasting requires resources commensurate with the goal.

System Standard E

SYSTEM STANDARD E
Science education policies must be equitable.

Science must be available to all students. To achieve this end, policies enacted toward that goal must likewise be equitable. Whether for reasons of economic or social disenfranchisement, ethnicity, gender, or school assignment, it is a fundamental educational right that all students have access to experiences in science that help them engage in the content, the processes, and the potential for social action promised by the best science curriculum and practices.

✓ Try This! 6–4   *Beyond the Classroom: Equity in Science Education*

SUPPORTING SCIENCE EDUCATION SYSTEM STANDARD E

Pick three school districts in your state—a rural one, a suburban one, and an urban one. How much money does it cost to educate pupils on a per-pupil basis? What are the different needs of students in these schools? Where is the per-pupil money actually spent? If you have an opportunity to follow up with an interview with teachers in these districts, find out what resources they have and what resources they wish they had to teach their students.

Based on your findings from this research, how would you respond to the statement "equal is not always equitable"?

System Standard F

Vigilance and reflection is the key here. This system standard is a very real concern in our post–*No Child Left Behind* era and its call for high-stakes testing. With our primary goal of helping all students engage in science and scientific ways of thinking, this can be subverted by the equally valid goal of regular testing of students to see what they have learned. Time and resources spent carrying out and assessing high-stakes testing can direct resources away from the principle goal of teaching students. While the testing issue is only one area of concern, the first point regarding vigilance is how the various elements of reform influence each other.

> **SYSTEM STANDARD F**
>
> All policy instruments must be reviewed for possible unintended effects on the classroom practice of science education.

Impact of No Child Left Behind

Description: The No Child Left Behind (NCLB) Act of 2001 represents the most significant education bill since the passage of the Elementary and Secondary Education Act in 1965.

> The law sets deadlines for states to expand the scope and frequency of student testing, revamp their accountability systems and guarantee that every teacher is qualified in their subject area. NCLB requires states to make demonstrable annual progress in raising the percentage of students proficient in reading and math, and in narrowing the test-score gap between advantaged and disadvantaged students. At the same time, the new law increases funding in several areas, including K–3 reading programs and before- and after-school programs, and provides states with greater flexibility to use federal funds as they see fit. (Education Commission of the States, 2004, paragraph 2)

The *Federal Register* (2002, p. 10167) summarized the goals for state accountability in NCLB:

- All students will reach high standards, at a minimum attaining proficiency or better in reading and mathematics by 2013–2014.
- By 2013–014, all students will be proficient in reading by the end of the third grade.
- All limited English proficient students will become proficient in English.
- By 2005–2006, all students will be taught by highly qualified teachers.
- All students will be educated in learning environments that are safe, drug free, and conducive to learning.
- All students will graduate from high school.

Impact: The effect of NCLB on education was immediate. In science education, a number of resources that were previously directed toward teacher improvement in the sciences (the former Eisenhower Grants) have been eliminated, and, as stated in the description above, most efforts toward implementation are now directed toward ensuring that schools make adequate yearly progress in the test scores that students receive in reading and mathematics. States are responding to the requirements of NCLB by directing additional resources to support the areas currently measured as an indicator of making adequate yearly progress. Beginning in 2007, science will be added to the content areas to be assessed in NCLB. Concerns have arisen among some science teachers and science educators that the incentive to perform well on tests will produce an instructional shift away from inquiry-based science instruction and toward more direct-instruction oriented experiences (Cavanaugh, 2004).

In terms of requiring "highly qualified" instructors for areas of academic content, science teachers in rural districts now (as of 2004) only have to demonstrate that they are "highly qualified" in a single area of content, rather than in all the areas they might be called upon to teach. However, each state can decide how to apply this requirement to the needs of students and teachers in their states.

Critique: Discussions surrounding NCLB have been quite heated at times. Recognizing that the expectations and timelines were, in some cases, onerous, Education Secretary Margaret Spellings announced rules that give greater flexibility in terms of how states may report the data required for NCLB (U.S. Department of Education, 2004). Some educators have stated that this most recent change provided evidence that the entire NCLB-mandated approach is unworkable and ultimately damaging to children and schools.

General critiques focus on the purpose for NCLB and the methodology employed. Regarding the purpose for NCLB, it is considered by some to be an inappropriate intrusion of the federal government into local school control. A more philosophical critique from authors such as Torres (2005) see it as a profound shift toward the ultimate privatizing of education, as states' inability to meet ever-increasing thresholds for scores to meet adequate yearly progress are part of "a larger political and ideological effort to privatize social programs, reduce the public sector, and ultimately replace local control of institutions like schools with marketplace reforms that substitute commercial relations between customers for democratic relations between citizens" (paragraph 26).

The inappropriate and punitive nature of testing (Neill, 2003) is the second broad critique of NCLB, with the intrusive nature of testing having the potential of forcing teachers to "teach to the test." These concerns were given voice in the wake of cheating scandals in Texas, the state that gave rise to President Bush and his advocacy for high-stakes testing of children. Benton and Hacker (2004) found highly suspect evidence in the form of increases in Adequate Yearly Progress in over 200 school districts that took the required TAKS examination. The suspect scores included among them a school that was recognized as "a National Blue Ribbon School that . . . was touted by federal officials as an example of top academic achievement" (paragraph 5).

While the Texas cheating scandal could be an isolated incident, it does offer one tangible consequence of high-stakes testing creating situations in which teachers and administrators make poor choices.

Responses to critics of NCLB include the House Committee on Education and the Workforce. It goes beyond the scope of this book to address all of the issues surrounding NCLB, but results cited by the House Committee (http://edworkforce.house.gov/nclb.htm) suggest NCLB is working in some settings. As a science teacher, the best advice that can be offered now is to apply the inquiry-based practices advocated in the National Science Education Standards to your own learning about No Child Left Behind: examine the data and its quality, consider the quality (and motivation) of the source material, and examine how the practices advocated as a consequence of NCLB influence your ability to teach science to your students.

System Standard G

Leadership is needed to begin making these changes a reality. Leadership from teachers, administrators, parents, legislators, and policy makers is essential to make genuine inquiry a reality in America's classrooms.

The role of teachers cannot be overstated. Their role in implementing the changes envisioned by the Standards makes them the most critical players in this shift in science teaching practice.

SYSTEM STANDARD G

Responsible individuals must take the opportunity afforded by the standards-based reform movement to achieve the new vision of science education portrayed in the Standards.

Science educators—that is, those who prepare teachers to teach science—have an important role in helping prospective and practicing teachers become more proficient in the implementation of inquiry-oriented practices in teaching science. The challenge here is profound, as most of today's prospective teachers have had very little opportunity to experience school-based science from the perspective of conducting inquiry. Given the "alien" quality of this experience, it is imperative that science educators make a case for teaching through inquiry and model those practices themselves.

Implications for Practice

The vision for science education systems is to have a coherent, inquiry-based instructional program supported by the various stakeholders throughout the system. Teachers, parents, school administrators, school boards, and those who have an interest in science and the preparation of science teachers have an obligation to work together. Supported by the vision of the Standards, working together—while never easy—is at least informed by a comprehensive vision of inquiry-based science experiences for all students.

The message of this chapter has been to emphasize the need for all parties to work together to support science instruction. Many people and institutions have had a vision of working to improve science teaching, but what has become clear over the decades is that significant and long-lasting change must come from orchestrated and well-planned change involving *all* of the parties involved in instruction—at all levels.

CLASSROOM SNAPSHOTS

NSES-Informed Science Education System Experiences

After five years as a teacher, Matt decided to pursue a graduate degree in science education to improve his teaching skills and meet his own personal goal of promoting inquiry in the classroom. During the summer of his graduate program, he helped his major professor deliver a series of science education workshops to support practicing elementary teachers as they sought to teach science through a process of inquiry. The project was implemented in four phases, each involving one or more of the constituencies represented in Project STICK: Science Teaching through Inquiry for Content Knowledge.

Phase I: Development of Content Knowledge

Fifty teachers were invited to participate in the staff development project. A six-weekend staff development training period was conducted at a Northern State University site by the two-person team of science educators from NSU, using physical science content staff development materials with a strong "learning through inquiry" focus. Primary teachers were instructed in the study of the following three topics: simple machines and motion, matter and changes, and electricity and magnetism. These topics were selected because they represent appropriate content for grades K to 3 and because they represent an essential knowledge base for other physical science concepts. The following outcomes were achieved during the training period:

Teachers achieved a basic level of understanding of selected physical science concepts. This was accomplished through a series of inquiry-based workshops, in which the teachers were challenged to grapple with their content knowledge through a series of experiences designed to challenge their knowledge of the subject matter. Insofar as possible, the approach paralleled the constructivist approach to learning advocated by learning theorists, generating content knowledge for teachers that was developed through direct teacher inquiry.

Teachers developed a curriculum outline as a precursor to developing a complete instructional unit. This served the purpose of alerting them to classroom applications of the concepts they were developing during the content area workshops. The curriculum outline ranged from individual lessons to broadly conceived instructional units to individual activities to carry out in the classroom.

Each teacher received a stipend for their participation and completion of the curriculum outlines. The stipend served as both a motivator and a reward for their participation in the project. Funding was also made available for the teachers to purchase classroom supplies that would be required as they taught the lessons they created in their classrooms.

Phase II: Development of Science Pedagogy

The same staff development team identified in Phase I conducted a three-week follow-up workshop. The workshop was designed to achieve the following objectives:

Training was provided in the use of science process skills to create science units. To this end, the use of science process skills as one of the objectives of science learning was introduced, and activities introducing each of the skills was introduced and demonstrated through a teacher-inquiry-based activity. These goals were incorporated as instructional objectives in the unit in conjunction with the content knowledge goals developed during the content area workshops.

Training was provided in the use of authentic assessments as part of inquiry-based science units. This helped to develop the ability among teachers to create authentic and performance-based assessment. An added value in this element of the program was the ability to model contemporary assessment practices in the classroom for preservice teachers.

Training was provided for ways to enhance the curriculum component with an interdisciplinary philosophy of teaching. Recognizing that time for science-only instruction is sometimes a luxury in the elementary classroom, strategies for adopting an interdisciplinary approach to instruction was advocated, and teachers infused this into the instructional units that they developed.

The completed science units, based on the content of the workshops and the district science curriculum, were submitted at the end of the summer session. To further support the use of technology in the teaching of science, the Project STICK teachers posted the resulting units on the Internet for later access and use by preservice teachers. Each teacher received three graduate semester hours of university credit and a stipend for successfully completing the physical science curriculum component.

Phase III: Implementation

During the fall semester, juniors majoring in elementary education received instruction using the inquiry-based philosophy of teaching physical science. They learned firsthand how the constructivist philosophy is used and how it can be applied in a primary classroom. Twenty-five preservice teachers were assigned to work with the half of the Project STICK teachers who developed the curriculum components in Phase II. Together, they team-taught the physical science lessons in the primary teacher's resident classroom. Among the specialized activities, most Project STICK mentor teachers required the preservice teachers to develop authentic assessment instruments to use in support of the science lessons developed during the summer workshops.

Project STICK teachers focused on mentoring the student teachers under their supervision. They demonstrated the effective teaching of science in a manner consistent with theory-supported notions of best practice, as well as using the content knowledge they developed over the summer to organize instruction and help their preservice teachers learn how to think about science in such a way as to make it more meaningful.

To this end, Project STICK teachers served as role models of exemplary science teaching for preservice teachers and supported this role by team-teaching their physical science curriculum unit with a preservice teacher. This served as a means of modeling the best practices of science teaching with the preservice teacher. It also provided a safety net to the starting teacher as he or she grappled with the significant issues and challenges of teaching in an inquiry-based classroom environment. To provide feedback and continuity, the university supervisor served as both the science methods instructor— a role taken on by Matt as part of his graduate work—for the preservice teachers as well as the workshop facilitator for the Project STICK teachers.

Phase IV: Further Implementation

The same sequence outlined in Phase III was repeated during the following spring semester. In this phase, a new group of preservice teachers worked with the remaining elementary teachers who were part of the Project STICK cadre.

Summary

As before, the experience recounted above was drawn from actual university and classroom practice, building a bridge between teachers, teacher educators, and preservice students. What set this experience apart from many summer workshops for teachers was the means by which multiple stakeholders were involved in the process. By increasing the professional skills of the classroom teachers— both in terms of content knowledge and science-based pedagogy—teachers in the project served as real leaders and reformers. Involvement by the university faculty who hosted and organized the workshop helped them to share their expertise, while at the same time connecting them to both teachers and elementary students during their classroom visits during the fall and spring semesters.

References

Bartels, D. M. (1999). An introduction to the National Science Education Standards. *Foundations, 2*, 15–23. Washington, DC: National Science Foundation.

Benton, J. K. & Hacker, M. K. (2004, December 30). Exclusive: Poor schools' TAKS surges raise cheating questions. *Dallas Morning News*. Retrieved on November 26, 2005, from http://www.dallasnews.com/sharedcontent/dws/dn/education/stories/121904dnmetcheating.64fa3.html

Benton, J. (2004, December 19). Tools may stem cheating on tests. *Dallas Morning News*. Retrieved on November 26, 2005, from http://www.dallasnews.com/sharedcontent/dws/dn/education/stories/122004dnmetcheating.4c687.html

Carin, A. A., Bass, J. E., & Contant, T. L. (2005). *Methods for teaching science as inquiry, 9th* ed. Upper Saddle River, NJ: Pearson Merrill Prentice Hall.

Cavanaugh, S. (2004, November 10). NCLB could alter science teaching. Retrieved on November 26, 2005, from http://www.aeoe.org/news/online/nclb-science-edweek111004.html

Decision Development Incorporated. (2000). Correlation to the national science education standards. Retrieved on May 6, 2004, from http://www.ddc2000.com/products/samples/s2kwebdemo/support/data/ unit00/00know/00003003.htm

Digital Library for Earth Science Education (2004). Student-teacher-scientist partnerships. Retrieved on June 3, 2004, from http://swiki.dlese.org/ReportOut2003/34

Education Commission of the States. (2004). ECS: No child left behind. Retrieved on November 26, 2005, from http://nclb2.ecs.org/Projects_Centers/index.aspx?issueid=gen&IssueName=General

Federal Register. (2002, March 6). Department of Education notices, *67*(44), 10166.

Fermi National Accelerator Laboratory. (2004). Fermilab today. Retrieved on June 3, 2004, from http://www.fnal.gov/pub/today/archive_2004/today04-04-27.html

National Society for the Study of Education. (1960). *Fifty-ninth yearbook: Rethinking science education.* Chicago: University of Chicago Press.

National Board for Professional Teaching Standards. (2004). Fields of certification: Certificates at a glance. Retrieved on May 6, 2004, from http://www.nbpts.org/candidates/guide/2_certglance.html

National Education Association. (2004). Teacher and paraprofessional quality. Retrieved on May 7, 2004, from http://www.nea.org/esea/eseateach.html

National Research Council. (1996). *National Science Education Standards.* National Academy Press: Washington, DC.

Neill, M. (2003). Don't mourn, organize! Retrieved on November 26, 2005, from http://www.rethinkingschools.org/special_reports/bushplan/nclb181.shtml

Origins Archive. (1996). Introduction to evolutionary biology. Retrieved on May 4, 2004, from http://www.talkorigins.org/faqs/faq-intro-to-biology.html

Science Curriculum, Inc. (no date). How introductory physical science & force, motion, and energy correlate to state and national standards. Retrieved on May 6, 2004, from http://www.sci-ips.com/correlations.html

Sokolove, P. G. (1999). The challenge of teaching biology 100: Can I *really* promote active learning in a large lecture? In M. B. Gardner, (Ed.), *Journeys of transformation: A statewide effort to improve mathematics and science professors to improve student understanding,* (pp. 121–128). (ERIC Document Reproduction Service No. ED467603).

Torres, C. (2005). No child left behind: A brainchild of neoliberalism and American politics. *New Politics, X*(2). Retrived on November 26, 2005, from http://www.wpunj.edu/~newpol/issue38/torres38.htm

U. S. Department of Education (2002). *No child left behind.* Washington, DC: Author.

U. S. Department of Education (2004). Spellings announces new special education guidelines, details workable, "common-sense" policy to help states implement no child left behind. Retrieved on November 26, 2005, from http://www.ed.gov/news/pressreleases/2005/05/05102005.html

Worth, K. (1999). The power of children's thinking. *Foundations, 2,* 25–37. Washington, DC: National Science Foundation.

CHAPTER 7

Standards for Professional Development for Teachers of Science

CLASSROOM SNAPSHOTS

As Mrs. Blue entered the school building, she waved to her colleagues, a number of whom were already gathered around the coffee, juice, and bagels, discussing a range of topics that extended from the new homework policy handed down by the assistant principal to the textbook decisions that were due in a few week's time. Teachers seemed to be intentionally avoiding discussing the day ahead, regarding it with the same degree of anticipation as one would regard a tax audit.

Mrs. Blue reflected on the program for the day, silently chewing her bagel, while her eyes ran over the program for the day's in-service program. The opening session on "Wellness for the Stressed-Out Teacher" bore the stamp of the school's new assistant principal. While Mrs. Blue recognized the need for managing stress among teachers, having the session imposed on her colleagues and herself was enough to make the bagel lose its taste. The next session, starting ninety minutes later, covered a completely different topic: how to make the state reading standards come alive in everyone's classroom. The lack of connection between the two topics and the fact that these would keep her busy until noon that day encouraged Mrs. Blue to wryly observe that perhaps the stress session was a good idea after all. All in all, at least there might be some use for these sessions, and they were both an improvement over the "Getting Along with Your Colleagues" session the previous semester.

Mrs. Blue found a seat near the rear of the auditorium and sat down with a group of her science department colleagues. As first-year teachers, they still demonstrated the enthusiasm and optimism that she recalled from her first year as a teacher, eight years earlier. She wondered what sort of teaching skills and methodologies they had been exposed to since she received her undergraduate degree. That would be a good topic for a long-term staff development initiative—becoming a better science teacher appealed to her. Learning how to apply the performance-based assessments that her newer colleagues did so well was of interest to her—as well as so much more. "Perhaps," she reflected, "this would be something to suggest on the evaluation form that I will turn in at the end of the day's program."

Her thoughts were interrupted by a scattered round of applause as the first speaker was introduced by the assistant principal. "Here we go!" stage-whispered one of her veteran colleagues. "I remember this presenter from about 1982!" The stage thus set, Mrs. Blue listened absently to the presenter and looked ahead eight weeks to the start of summer vacation.

Introduction

Depending on if you are reading this chapter as a teacher-to-be or as an experienced educator, you will likely have different reactions to the potential offered by an in-service or staff development day. As a new teacher or preservice teacher, the potential to develop new skills and increase skill in the classroom makes the possibility of further professional development seem attractive. For those teachers who, as the characters in the opening vignette represent, it can be a frustrating time when programs are imposed externally that seem to have little to do with helping students to learn.

As you will see as you read this chapter, the potential for significant professional growth is truly a part of a staff development experience. But, for this to become a reality, the teacher needs to be a part of the experience, from design through implementation—and be supported by administrators who understand this as well. This chapter will give you tools to help make staff development a day to look forward to in your life as a teacher—and help you to look for opportunities to be a part of the process of improving your own professional expertise.

Changing Emphases

Nearly fifty years ago, the National Society for the Study of Education (NSSE) devoted the content of one of their annual yearbooks to the need for in-service education. Since that time, "in-service" has become a verb and is not perceived in flattering terms by many teachers. The need for such ongoing support for teachers was laid out in this manner:

> That there is great need for better programs of in-service education is rarely contested. [O]ur rapidly changing culture and its implication for curriculum change, the continuing increase in pupil enrollments and numbers of teachers, . . . the continuous additions to our knowledge in general and particularly our knowledge about children and youth and the learning process, all, in cumulation, mean that professional school people need to work continuously to keep abreast of what they must know and must be able to do. (NSSE, 1957, p. 1)

The NSSE's 1957 document focused, however, on a needs analysis and implementation approach that was analyzed and implemented from a central administrative authority. While no one would disagree with the *reasons* cited for continuing professional development for teachers, the recognition that teachers need to be involved intimately with the design, development, and delivery of such programs is better realized now than it was in the 1950s. Our motivation as educators remains the same, while our ability to implement such changes more effectively has improved.

The National Society for the Study of Education also looked at the specific needs of science teachers during the same era (NSSE, 1960). The focus during

TABLE 7.1   Changing Emphases for Professional Development*

Less Emphasis On	More Emphasis On
Transmission of teaching knowledge and skills by lectures	Inquiry into teaching and learning
Learning science by lecture and reading	Learning science through investigation and inquiry
Separation of science and teaching knowledge	Integration of science and teaching knowledge
Separation of theory and practice	Integration of theory and practice in school settings
Individual learning	Collegial and collaborative learning
Fragmented, one-shot sessions	Long-term coherent plans
Courses and workshops	A variety of professional development activities
Reliance on external expertise	Mix of internal and external expertise
Staff developers as educators	Staff developers as facilitators, consultants, and planners
Teacher as technician	Teacher as intellectual, reflective practitioner
Teacher as consumer of knowledge about teaching	Teacher as producer of knowledge about teaching
Teacher as follower	Teacher as leader
Teacher as an individual based in a classroom	Teacher as a member of a collegial professional community
Teacher as target of change	Teacher as source and facilitator of change

*Reprinted with permission from *National Science Education Standards* © 1996 by the National Academy of Sciences, courtesy of the National Academies Press, Washington, DC, p. 72.

that time was on the acquisition of more content knowledge and the challenge teachers faced in "keeping up" with ever-increasing amounts of scientific knowledge then being produced. If anything is true, the issue of greater and greater amounts of content knowledge available to be transmitted to students has increased by orders of magnitude. Again, as part of an era during which these needs were first identified, the approach given to serve teacher's professional needs was primarily from a top-down perspective. The changing emphases in standards related to professional development underscore the practices for effective staff development that have been implemented in the decades since the NSSE made their case for improving staff development. These changes are summarized in Table 7.1.

The emphasis now makes clear the important role teachers must have in their own staff development needs and roles. Rather than being the recipients of knowledge, it is hoped that teachers will be successful as a resource for other teachers, as well as key figures in the process of developing more knowledge and determining what knowledge is required to successfully educate youth in the twenty-first century.

Examining and Interpreting the Professional Development Standards

The standards supporting the professional development of teachers assume that teachers are more than simply technicians who will be implementing a curriculum determined by others and then handed down to the teachers to implement. The focus of the skills and the approach advocated by the National

Science Education Standards is that teachers are well-trained, competent, and thoughtful professionals. The experiences and competencies outlined among these standards seek to promote long-term professional development among teachers.

The Standards also recognize the high level of responsibility teachers have for their own staff development. Just as we look at teaching as an interactive process with students and teachers working together to build knowledge, the vision represented by the Standards is that teachers likewise have a professional obligation and commitment to build and develop their own understanding of the content they will be delivering. With this mission in mind, teachers then must seek the best and most appropriate means of delivering such information.

Professional Development Standard A

One of the great challenges of becoming an effective science teacher is to learn how to *do* science. Most instruction teachers receive focuses on learning *about* science. While this achieves a healthy "Monday morning quarterback" appreciation of science, there is no substitute for doing the real thing. This presents challenges in the preparation of many teachers, especially for those in elementary programs whose main preparation is that of a generalist. Keep in mind, however, that all teachers engage in writing and they teach writing as well. All teachers (hopefully) vote, and emphasize the responsibilities of citizenship. In the same way, seeking out opportunities to engage in the pursuit of knowledge in a manner consistent with the elements of science should be a part of their preparation.

Part of teacher preparation has often been a response to the question, "What makes science teaching 'good'?" A better question might be, what makes science teaching *effective*? The consensus among science educators has been captured well in the American Association for the Advancement of Science's (AAAS) (1989) *Science for all Americans*. Essential elements of science teaching include the recognition that what and how students learn is influenced by their

---

PROFESSIONAL DEVELOPMENT STANDARD A

Professional development for teachers of science requires learning essential science content through the perspectives and methods of inquiry. Science learning experiences for teachers must

- Involve teachers in actively investigating phenomena that can be studied scientifically, interpreting results, and making sense of findings consistent with currently accepted scientific understanding.
- Address issues, events, problems, or topics significant in science and of interest to participants.
- Ground the work in current learning and pedagogical theory and practices.
- Introduce teachers to scientific literature, media, and technological resources that expand their science knowledge and their ability to access further knowledge.
- Build on the teacher's current science understanding, ability, and attitudes.
- Incorporate ongoing reflection on the process and outcomes of understanding science through inquiry.
- Encourage and support teachers in efforts to collaborate.

✔ Try This! 7–1 *Teachers' Perceptions on Professional Development*

SUPPORTING PROFESSIONAL DEVELOPMENT STANDARD A

Interview a teacher and gain their insights into the professional development experiences they have had. After your interview, compare their responses to the information in Table 7.1, Changing Emphases for Professional Development. Visit with them after the interview and share with them how their remarks correspond to the evolving standards for professional development. What is their reaction to finding their comments compared to a set of evolving standards? Do they agree with your classification/interpretation of their remarks?

existing ideas. In terms of learning theory advanced by Piaget, (Inhelder & Piaget, 1964) this theory is related to issues of accommodation and assimilation—how new knowledge and experiences interact with existing schema. Another general principle is that ideas are most appropriately formed when the learner moves from concrete experiences toward abstraction. The ability to manipulate materials before manipulating ideas helps people organize their ideas—and guards against our tendency as teachers to overemphasize the use of lecture and spoken language lessons to the exclusion of investigations that begin with interactions with tangible objects.

Two additional points noted by AAAS: people are more successful at tasks they can practice and effective learning is built upon useful feedback. The importance of the former is that science is, for many people, a genuinely novel experience. With this novelty comes the need for teachers to help learners practice these new skills and new ways of thinking, which leads to the second point: learning requires meaningful feedback. The real value of feedback is more than just marking the correct answers on a test sheet; the real value of feedback comes from sharing evaluative information with the learner, so that he or she can try again with the feedback in place, continuously building, testing, and rebuilding their knowledge.

The final point regarding effective science teaching supports *all* teaching: expectations influence performance. When there is a lack of confidence in one's ability to be successful, it can be the start of a continuous cycle of failure. A responsible teacher helps to build success in learning by having high expectations for success, helping learners recognize their own success, and assist them in building confidence in their capacity to learn.

The principles of effective science teaching are easy enough to commit to memory, so why is there such criticism of science teaching in the United States? What differentiates experienced teachers from novice teachers, and how does meaningful experience serve to help teachers become successful?

Crave (2002) noted that the available research on how novice teachers and expert teachers deliver instruction depends to a large degree on how they cognitively organize their understanding of a discipline. Quoting the work of Novik:

> Laura Novik conducted an experiment in which she looked at the ability of experts in certain domains to teach novices how to complete an analytical problem. She found some very interesting results. Her findings were consistent with her hypotheses that experts represent and store information in different ways than novices. This makes it difficult to transfer expert knowledge. Novik found that novices remember different information than experts when reviewing a problem. Novices represent salient surface features such as specific objects and terms mentioned, whereas experts represent both surface and structural features in order to solve the stated problem. This means that experts are able to represent and store more complex information than novices, which is more helpful in solving the problem. Novik's study shows that an expert cognitively represents information and knowledge differently than the novice. Expert teachers, who have tacit knowledge of what effective teaching is, have represented this information in a way that a novice would not understand due to the complex and tacit nature of it. The novice concentrates on the apparent and surface features while the expert looks deeper at the structure of the problem posed. (paragraph 2)

Other authors echo these perspectives. Shulman, in particular, has written extensively on what teachers know and how they need to understand their discipline in order to teach effectively. Garmston (1998) notes that there are six elements to effective teaching that are supported by research:

1. Content knowledge (structure of the discipline)
2. Effective pedagogy, connected to knowledge of the discipline

3. Knowledge of students and how they learn
4. Teacher self-knowledge (including values, standards, and beliefs)
5. Cognitive processes of instruction
6. Collegial interaction (paragraphs 4–10)

The final point—collegial interaction—is an essential element of the staff development experience. It makes the difference between staff development that is done *to* a professional and professional development that *involves* the teacher. The message present in the NSES is staff development can be a means for supporting collegial interactions. The framework for action the Standards offer is built on the notion that teachers have an essential role in planning their own staff development experiences.

For most teachers, whether working with primary, intermediate, or secondary students, the first post-high school introduction to what science is comes from the introductory remarks in science content courses they take as part of their bachelor's degree program. Methods courses in science generally focus on the process of inquiry and the development of an appreciation and understanding of the nature of science, and how science can be implemented in a meaningful way in the classroom.

As student teachers move into the ranks of professional teachers, the challenge of implementing this knowledge in a systematic and meaningful way becomes critical. Seeking professional development experiences that focus on the development of inquiry skills and attitudes provides a means of helping teachers share with their students a respect for *doing* science rather than approaching it as a spectator sport.

Far too often, staff development programs fail to help their participants engage in experiences that "[a]ddress issues, events, problems, or topics significant in science and of interest to participants" (National Academy of Sciences, 1996, p. 59). Having the needs of teachers determined externally does not develop the professionalism of teachers. Beyond the issue of professionalism, determining their own needs for staff development is an important part of the process of personal and professional growth for teachers. Changing times, changes in local circumstances, and changes in course content are all issues that the classroom teacher knows intimately, and the ability to craft and develop professional development programs around those needs is necessary for staff development to move from perfunctory to meaningful.

Effective staff development models have multiple elements in place to support the long-term needs of teachers, students, and the system in which they reside. The North Central Regional Educational Laboratory, part of the Department of Education's Institute of Education Sciences, offers a synthesis of effective staff development practices (Hassel, 1999, Cited in North Central Educational Research Laboratory, 2004). Among the key elements are the following:

- Include participants in the design process
- Ensure that the professional development plan is consistent with the school or school district's values and long-term planning
- Conduct a needs assessment to ensure that staff development is addressing a professional development need, rather than delivering a program because it is available, convenient, or cheap
- Identify professional development goals for the faculty
- Define the process, goals, and staff development activities
- Ensure that a sound research base informs the staff development program

- Identify and ensure that resources are in place to support the staff development plan and its implementation
- Plan the process and ensure that the professional community is apprised of the plans North Central Regional Education Laboratory. (NCREL, 2004, paragraph 5)

✓ Try This! 7–2 *Administrator's Perceptions of Staff Development Experiences*

SUPPORTING PROFESSIONAL DEVELOPMENT STANDARD A

Using the points developed above (NCREL, 2004), interview a principal in your building or a science department chair. In what way do they see the key issues for effective staff development being implemented in their building?

Follow up the administrator interview by interviewing a teacher and asking them to respond to the same points. Share with your class what you found. Do the administrators and teachers see things in the same way, or are there some differences? If they are the same, what is in place in that school to give all parties a common vision of effective implementation of staff development? If there are differences, what might account for these differences?

Beyond mastering specific new knowledge and pedagogy as part of the staff development process, the need for teachers to become better and more aware consumers of knowledge is an important part of the process. The idea of ongoing staff development through professional literature has expanded dramatically since the time of *Rethinking Science Education* (National Society for the Study of Education, 1960). At that time, only a handful of journals were available to meet the needs of science teachers. Today, information is available from a wide variety of sources, including both national organizations and their state affiliates, but also raw information is available through telecommunications and listserv functions. Access to information has never been greater, and teachers can find assistance for the teaching of science arriving daily in their electronic mailboxes. Listservs, in particular, offer the teacher an opportunity to be *part* of the staff development process, as their expertise can be shared efficiently with others in the electronic community.

SUPPORTING PROFESSIONAL DEVELOPMENT STANDARD A: LESSON 7.1

Refining Your Practice: Professional Development Organizations

Professional Organizations for Science Teachers. There are a variety of professional organizations for science teachers. Internet access and e-mail have served to make them more responsive and more available than ever before. Visit one or more and find out what resources they can provide to you as a teacher.

- American Association of Physics Teachers: http://www.aapt.org/
- American Association for Health Education: http://www.aahperd.org/aahe/
- Association of Science–Technology Centers: http://www.astc.org/
- American Chemical Society: http://www.chemistry.org
- Association for the Advancement of Computers in Education: http://www.aace.org/
- Association for Educational Communications and Technology: http://www.aect.org/
- Association for Supervision and Curriculum Development: http://www.ascd.org
- International Society for Technology in Education: http://www.iste.org/

- National Council for Teachers of Mathematics: http://www.nctm.org/
- National Association of Biology Teachers: http://www.nabt.org/
- National Earth Science Teachers Association: http://www.nestanet.org/
- National Association of Geoscience Teachers: http://www.nagt.org/nagt/index.html
- National Science Teachers Association: http://www.nsta.org/
- School Science and Mathematics: http://www.ssma.org/
- Society for the Advancement of Chicanos & Native Americans in Science: http://www.sacnas.org/
- National Association for Research in Science Teaching: http://www.educ.sfu.ca/narstsite/
- National Staff Development Council: http://www.nsdc.org/
- Association of Science Teacher Educators: http://aste.chem.pitt.edu/
- American Association for the Advancement of Science: http://www.aaas.org/
- National Academy of Sciences: http://www.nas.edu/
- National Science Foundation: http://www.nsf.gov/
- U.S. Department of Education: http://www.ed.gov/index.jhtml

Regardless of the structure of staff development, whether it be one-on-one conversations, a summer institute, a graduate program of study, or e-mails from interested colleagues, the knowledge must build on what the teacher already knows. Piaget's concepts of assimilation and accommodation are not only constructs for building knowledge in children: they are a foundation for adult learning as well. The development of new knowledge and skills must be constructed on the intellectual foundation of the classroom teacher and be perceived to meet his or her needs. Clearly, this can be done best when the teacher is part of the staff development process, rather than a passive recipient of whatever knowledge is deemed to be important by administrators.

Try This! 7–3   *Writing for Learning and Publication*

SUPPORTING PROFESSIONAL DEVELOPMENT STANDARD A

One strategy for building reflection into the professional development process is to write about one's experiences. Writing can help to process and organize one's thoughts, and it can also provide an opportunity to share skills and expertise with other educators. In addition to organizing one's thoughts and communicating your activities to a new audience, part of the process of professional writing often involves connecting your new work and experiences with a theoretical base or with other work done in the same area.

Science teaching journals exist for a variety of audiences: *Science and Children, Science Scope, The Science Teacher, Science Activities,* and others solicit examples of teaching, assessment, staff development, and other practices from teachers. A recent issue of *The Science Teacher* (a journal for secondary science teachers) shared a variety of activities profiling student-teacher-community interactions, showing how teachers implemented standards-based instruction for their students, while working with community agencies and resources. A recent issue of *Science and Children* (a journal for elementary teachers with an interest in teaching science) profiled a variety of strategies for teaching force and motion concepts to young children.

All of these journals support standards-based practices, and all seek contributions from practicing teachers who have worthy ideas to share with their colleagues. The first step toward one's reflective staff development might be as close as a pad of paper and a pen.

Staff development must also incorporate collaboration among teachers as one of its foundational principles. Building communities of learners can—and should—be one of the key outcomes of professional development. Promoting a staff development model in which teachers work together to learn, to solve problems, and to promote scholarship and growth among their students and themselves is the final piece in staff development that engages all participants, rather than staff development that is dictated by outside sources. Whether this community is within a science department, within a school building of elementary teachers interested in science teaching, or an electronic community operated through a listserv, this approach promotes collaboration and community.

Professional Development Standard B

Science is more than content knowledge. It is a blend of experiences, skills, attitudes, and curiosity. Science teaching is more than passing on accumulated wisdom through overhead transparencies or simply the honorable, but ultimately inappropriate, task of imitating one's professor in front of a group of P–12 students. Teaching science involves knowledge of content, understanding how students think and learn, and process skill knowledge—interact to create a specialized form of knowledge known as pedagogical content knowledge. (Schulman, 1986; Smith, 2000). Pedagogical content knowledge includes

> **PROFESSIONAL DEVELOPMENT STANDARD B**
>
> Professional development for teachers of science requires integrating knowledge of science, learning, pedagogy, and students; it also requires applying that knowledge to science teaching. Learning experiences for teachers of science must
>
> - Connect and integrate all pertinent aspects of science and science education.
> - Occur in a variety of places where effective science teaching can be illustrated and modeled, permitting teachers to struggle with real situations and expand their knowledge and skills in appropriate contexts.
> - Address teachers' needs as learners and build on their current knowledge of science content, teaching, and learning.
> - Use inquiry, reflection, interpretation of research, modeling, and guided practice to build understanding and skill in science teaching.

the most useful forms of representation of [topics], the most powerful analogies, illustrations, examples, explanations, and demonstrations—in a word, the ways of representing and formulating the subject that make it comprehensible to others. . . . Pedagogical content knowledge also includes an understanding of what makes the learning of specific topics easy or difficult: the conceptions and preconceptions that students of different ages and backgrounds bring with them to the learning of those most frequently taught topics and lessons. (Herr, 2001, paragraph 2)

Herr summarizes pedagogical content knowledge as a combination of interrelated elements, primarily a general knowledge of instruction within the framework of the curriculum, the sorts of naïve concepts held by students, and a knowledge of how children form concepts—all aided by the deep knowledge of a teacher's subject area of expertise. Pedagogical content knowledge helps teachers use their knowledge and skills effectively. Knowing how students construct knowledge in a scientific context and understanding the challenges and obstacles to learning that students experience while engaging in the learning of science are key areas that need to be addressed in the ongoing professional development of teachers.

Staff development need not take place only in a school auditorium. Nature centers, research laboratories, libraries, or teachers' classrooms can be appropriate settings for professional development, depending on the topic being addressed. For those who live close to governmental and industrial research laboratories, staff development experiences should utilize those resources. Government and university laboratories, such as Fermi National Accelerator Laboratory, Argonne National Laboratory, Columbia University Nevis Laboratories, the University of California, Berkeley, Sandia National Laboratory, Lawrence Berkeley National Laboratory, and others, offer resources and facilities that serve the professional development needs of K–12 science teachers. Contributing to the success of these laboratories in their staff development efforts is the knowledge of the scientists themselves—the "real" scientists who contribute their professional knowledge and help less experienced colleagues in education learn to think about science in ways that are similar to practicing scientists.

Collaborations among science teachers, their students, and researchers have been facilitated by the use of the Internet and other telecommunications tools. The QuarkNet Project allows teachers, students, and researchers to collaborate on particle physics research, developing the teacher's research skills and content knowledge simultaneously with those of their students. Other initiatives, such as Project GLOBE, provide for staff development in an equally transparent manner: students and teachers learn together in their pursuit of new knowledge, and staff development needs are met through solving problems in collaboration with their own students and practicing scientists.

 Try This! 7–4 *School–University Partnerships*

SUPPORTING PROFESSIONAL DEVELOPMENT STANDARD B

Professional relationships between schools and universities can offer excellent opportunities for staff development. Pursuing involvement in such a project can have tremendous positive effects on professional growth and development. In the best-designed and implemented experiences, the staff development experience involves all parties as equals in the relationship.

In studies on involvement in a partnership, Dodge (1993) identified and examined the extant research and noted that the presence of these elements makes for a successful relationship:

- Project goals should be jointly conceived and agreed upon.
- Teachers should be actively involved, not just passive recipients.
- If teachers are to be involved as equal partners, they must be involved for as much time as the other actors.
- Exchanges should be reciprocal; each partner should gain something. Education should be mutual; each party must develop an appreciation of the other's contribution.
- Leadership should rotate among partners as appropriate to their skills.
- Outcomes should be mutually owned. The university must be committed to the collaborative ideal and provide financial support if necessary, including stipends or load credit for faculty members. (p. 1)

As one hopes that a district's science curriculum considers student needs in the development of learning experiences, it is important that teachers' needs and knowledge likewise be taken into consideration in the development and implementation of their staff development programming. "One size fits all" barely works for ball caps—in no way does it meet the needs of all teachers.

"Use inquiry, reflection, interpretation of research, modeling, and guided practice to build understanding and skill in science teaching" (NSES, p. 62). Being an effective science teacher means more than developing deep content knowledge—it involves knowing how to organize one's content knowledge in such a way that it can be communicated to students.

Effective science teaching requires meaningful reflection upon one's practices. In Ferraro's (2000) summary of the research on reflective practice, she identified the following essential characteristics:

1. understand the context in which the reflection is taking place
2. ensure that the reflection is taking place within a broader conceptual framework (thus avoiding a "checklist" approach)
3. encourage reflection beyond current teaching practices and challenge current practice
4. engage in personal disclosure with respect to current teaching practices
5. encourage implementation as part of an ongoing program of staff development

Effective reflection on one's teaching practices can be accomplished through many means, including allowing a colleague to make observations of your teaching and provide thoughtful feedback. Much good can be accomplished by visiting other classrooms and watching other teachers at work. These ideas are far removed from the standard "one day–one shot" form of staff development commonly employed. Instead, they become ongoing, they encourage reflection and encourage growth on the part of the teacher, and they require that the teacher's needs are used to determine the type and arrangement of the staff development process. Improving one's practices as a teacher is at the heart of all staff development initiatives. As teaching has often been considered both art and science, the best way to actually produce measurable changes in teaching is to focus on the science part of teaching. The changes produced by focusing on the science of teaching are more consistent and reproducible than those connected with the ethereal art of teaching.

Berliner (1985) made observations two decades ago regarding the value of research in improving teaching practices, ranging from verifying existing ideas and identifying counterintuitive findings, to providing a sound pedagogical basis for practices that often antagonize the nonacademic community (e.g., the use of cooperative learning). More recent findings, documented in such volumes as *How People Learn* (National Research Council, 2000) offer further support for improving teaching practices, taking into consideration critical issues in the mind, the brain, and the role of experience.

PROFESSIONAL DEVELOPMENT STANDARD C

Professional development for teachers of science requires building understanding and ability for lifelong learning. Professional development activities must

- Provide regular, frequent opportunities for individual and collegial examination and reflection on classroom and institutional practice.
- Provide opportunities for teachers to receive feedback about their teaching and to understand, analyze, and apply that feedback to improve their practice.
- Provide opportunities for teachers to learn and use various tools and techniques for self-reflection and collegial reflection, such as peer coaching, portfolios, and journals.
- Support the sharing of teacher expertise by preparing and using mentors, teacher advisers, coaches, lead teachers, and resource teachers to provide professional development opportunities.
- Provide opportunities to know and have access to existing research and experiential knowledge.
- Provide opportunities to learn and use the skills of research to generate new knowledge about science and the teaching and learning of science.

Professional Development Standard C

Reflecting on practice is the first step toward making positive and proactive changes in teaching and learning. The maxim "no one needs to know what happens behind the closed classroom door" is a perspective that needs to be retired. Reflection for individuals seldom takes place as often as it should. Reflection among small groups of teachers likewise does not take place as frequently as it should; one of the primary obstacles is the institutional barriers that prevent such conversations from taking place.

Instructional leaders—department chairs, instructional coordinators, and principals—can respond to these needs by encouraging dialog and giving teachers the time to consider their own practice. As developing the knowledge required to deliver content and process skills effectively is acquired over time, the need to allow time for reflection and dialog is critical. Beyond encouraging time for reflection and networking among teaching colleagues, administrators should be arranging support through schedule adjustments and financial support for hiring substitute teachers while classroom teachers are engaged in professional development experiences.

A variety of tools for growth and reflection need to be part of the teacher's professional growth experiences. Self-reflection provides an excellent start for improving one's practice in the classroom. To move beyond this point, however, teachers need to have specific and focused feedback to help their teaching practice evolve. Danielson and McGreal (2000; Danielson, 1996) make clear that a variety of tools are needed and that teachers at various stages of their professional careers have specific needs that cannot be well addressed through large-group, one-size-fits-all in-service experiences. In particular, the needs of beginning teachers require processes of mentoring, of observations by both peers and supervisors, and of specific organized support systems. More experienced teachers, especially those in a new setting or school, will have vastly different professional development needs, and those need to be addressed by the system as well.

 Try This! 7–5   *Informing Your Professional Practice*

SUPPORTING PROFESSIONAL DEVELOPMENT STANDARD C

Technology offers the opportunity for teachers to examine their classroom practices. In a case study presented by Rolf Blank and Stan Hill, they demonstrate the use of the interactive *Surveys of Enacted Curriculum* (SEC) analysis tool (available at www.SECSurvey.org). This tool allows teachers to "compare their instruction with other teachers, schools, or districts, and to review the degree of alignment between local instruction and state standards and assessment" (p. 55).

Being able to identify current practices and compare them objectively with curriculum and assessment standards is a key step for improving science instruction. This allows teachers to examine their own practices as a first step in instruction improvement. The SEC tool allows teachers at all levels—elementary, middle school, and high school—to record their instructional practices, such as collecting information about science, maintaining a portfolio of science work, engaging in laboratory investigations, and so on.

The results can be compared to learning goals identified by state and local learning standards and can be further used to examine discrepancies between the desired teaching/learning practices and the actual experiences in the classroom. The SEC tool can also be used to compare practices within a single school or between different schools around the country.

Blank and Hill note three positive outcomes related to the use of this application, all supporting standards-based instruction, while honoring the real-world issues faced by teachers.

- The SEC gives real data directly to the teachers, allowing them to make informed instructional decisions about their own practice.
- The data is most useful when used by teams of teachers working collaboratively at improving their instruction and their students' learning.
- The SEC allows teachers to examine assessment data and to compare them with instructional practices–in essence, the SEC can serve as a diagnostic tool.

The SEC is one of several interactive software tools under development, but for the purposes of the Standards, it remains focused on science teaching.

From Blank and Hill (2004), "Analyzing Instructional Content and Practices."

More experienced teachers—including those who are tenured—can benefit from experiences such as classroom observations, teacher self-assessments, structured reflection, and student/parent/colleague feedback. Each of these provides specific information that can be used by the teacher as he or she develops professionally. Other supervision and staff development scholars (cf. Glickman, 2002) offer the same perspective: improving teaching and learning must be systematic in nature, especially with respect to meaningful, focused observations.

"Support the sharing of teacher expertise by preparing and using mentors" (NSES, p. 68) underscores the importance of a teacher's professional knowledge and the knowledge of his or her colleagues. While professional development, in terms of the relationship between the supervisor and the teacher, can range from highly supervisor-directed, to collaborative, to nondirective, the value of developing mentors from within a learning community is profound. This perspective on professional development is one of the keys to developing a genuine community that supports staff development *from* teachers, as opposed to having it inflicted upon them. Besides the intrinsic value of developing the skills of beginning teachers, it further helps to broaden and develop the skills of experienced teachers, as they share their expertise with their less experienced colleagues. Some local communities—especially in suburban areas—have created successful professional development groups, such as "Physics Northwest" for physics teachers in the northern and western suburbs of the Chicago metropolitan area. Other opportunities for professional development and mentors come from state science teaching organizations, typically those that are state affiliates of the National Science Teachers Association.

Gaining access to professional knowledge is an important element in a teacher's staff development process. Methods courses taken as undergraduate students are often regrettably forgotten as teachers move from their preservice years into their in-service experiences. An excellent means of support for teachers provided by administrators, supervisors, and experienced mentor teachers is identifying professional knowledge and connecting it with the in-service teacher's professional practice. Areas of content development and content enrichment are obvious areas for professional development. As discussed previously, content knowledge and an understanding of the processes of science can be part of a summer institute working with practicing scientists and researchers. Developing improved pedagogy in areas such as individualized instruction, special needs students, problem-based learning, and many other areas connects with the pedagogical skills required of exemplary teachers.

There is unfortunately a disconnect between what science teachers share during their classes and the types of real-world experiences they typically possess. Industrial arts teachers often have experience in woodworking or electricity. English teachers read, write, and use the language. Art teachers are often skilled sculptors or painters. Science teachers rarely have experience as practicing scientists. Obtaining access to the skills of science and research is an area that many science teachers would embrace. This does not imply that science teachers are necessarily ineffective because they have not worked as a scientist, but these experiences can provide a depth and perspective that benefits and enriches the classroom experience for both teachers and students.

Opportunities for teachers to take part in science experiences are available through business, government, and industry. Business concerns, especially those with engineering or manufacturing functions, often provide summer internships for teachers, sharing elements of the research and development process with them. Applications of scientific principles and, for those businesses with a research and development program, the ability to see "real" scientific investigations in progress provide perspective to teachers. The chance to participate in an investigation provides depth and perspective that strengthens their teaching practice. The school-university partnerships mentioned previously may offer another opportunity for teachers to engage in scientific research.

National laboratories often offer workshops or invite teachers to serve on a summer research team as part of their outreach programs. In some of these programs, teachers participate as team members, carrying out research along with the scientists employed by the agency.

The federal government also provides opportunities for teachers to be involved in scientific research. Programs such as TEA—Teachers Experiencing Antarctica and the Arctic—provide an opportunity for teachers to live for six to eight weeks as research assistants with scientists whose area of expertise is related to the Antarctic or Arctic. Programs like this involve not only secondary teachers, but elementary teachers as well.

> The centerpiece of the Teachers Experiencing Antarctica and the Arctic (TEA) Program is a research experience in which a K–12 teacher participates in a polar expedition. The TEA teacher works closely with scientists, participates in cutting-edge research, and is immersed in the process of science. Enveloping this field experience is a diversity of professional development opportunities through which TEA teachers increase content knowledge, enhance teaching skills, transfer the experience to the classroom, assume leadership roles, and collaborate with a network of researchers and education colleagues. TEA is a partnership between teachers, researchers, students, the school district, and the community. (TEA, 2003)

While projects like TEA are somewhat competitive, they are available for all teachers who develop the skills to participate—and for those who show the desire to participate. Projects like this also represent meaningful and significant forms of staff development, with the benefits meeting the needs of the teacher, his or her colleagues, students, and communities. Administrators and supervisors can be of help by keeping their science teaching colleagues informed of various opportunities and supporting them in their efforts to participate.

Professional Development Standard D

One of the purposes of the National Science Education Standards is to provide a comprehensive vision of everything that makes up "science education" in the United States. As the NSES provide a vision of what science education can look like, so must local districts and local organizations create their own comprehensive and meaningful vision of what professional development for teachers looks like.

The culture of individual schools and districts determines in large part where the responsibility for staff development lies—shared between teachers and administrators or with administrators alone (Nelson, Palonsky, & McCarthy, 2004). Regardless of who has the responsibility within a school or district, the worst staff development programs—the in-service experiences delivered by convenience—should be the first casualties of a comprehensive and articulated staff development program. Having a shared, coherent vision in place at the outset is the first step in a meaningful professional development process.

PROFESSIONAL DEVELOPMENT STANDARD D

Professional development programs for teachers of science must be coherent and integrated. Quality preservice and inservice programs are characterized by

- Clear, shared goals based on a vision of science learning, teaching, and teacher development congruent with the National Science Education Standards.
- Integration and coordination of the program components so that understanding and ability can be built over time, reinforced continuously, and practiced in a variety of situations.
- Options that recognize the developmental nature of teacher professional growth and individual and group interests, as well as the needs of teachers who have varying degrees of experience, professional expertise, and proficiency.
- Collaboration among the people involved in programs, including teachers, teacher educators, teacher unions, scientists, administrators, policy makers, members of professional and scientific organizations, parents, and business people, with clear respect for the perspectives and expertise of each.
- Recognition of the history, culture, and organization of the school environment.
- Continuous program assessment that captures the perspectives of all those involved, uses a variety of strategies, focuses on the process and effects of the program, and feeds directly into program improvement and evaluation.

Common goals provide the purpose for all staff development experiences. Staff development—professional development, actually—is a process that extends from one's start in a teacher education program to the end of one's professional practice. Fortunately, most methods courses in science are taught in a way that recognizes this, but they represent only the start of the process.

Staff development requires a variety of activities conducted over time. Multiple interrelated and articulated experiences can be developed to meet staff development needs. Having a variety of experiences over time allows teachers to have their skills enhanced. A continuum of experiences will benefit teachers from their preservice era through their in-service era; the experiences also need to include all teachers from K–12. This serves to create a community of teachers interested in developing meaningful, coherent science experiences for K–12 and, ideally, K–16.

Reflective practice is one of the critical elements of staff development and needs to be built into the process. Time to think about improving practice helps to develop teachers who consider change deeply, consider the consequences of their actions, and map out long-term strategies for growth and development, rather than simply reacting to instructional situations.

The developmental needs of beginning teachers during the induction phase of their professional career are vastly different from those of more experienced faculty members. Building a professional development community takes advantage of the expertise of veteran faculty members and builds their professional skills by helping them deliver staff development experiences to their less experienced colleagues.

One of the greatest challenges in producing meaningful staff development experiences is getting all relevant parties to work collaboratively. While all parties, from administrators to teacher union representatives, have the same goals in mind—an excellent education for students—the means by which those goals are achieved can often seem to be in conflict. All parties need to focus on their common interests and use those commonalties as the purpose for organizing professional development experiences. The value of multiple constituencies working to support science teaching lies not only in their common goal—improving learning for students—but also in the perspectives they bring to the common goal. Teachers bring knowledge of pedagogy, scientists bring content knowledge, administrators understand educational systems, and members of the business community have an interest in students eventually participating in the workforce.

Related to the common goals of staff development and teaching shared by these constituencies is an understanding of the school and its institutional needs, its culture, and its organization. Attempts to change and enhance teaching practices without considering the context and culture of the institution, if not quite doomed to failure, will certainly produce additional challenges. The outcome suggested here will help the culture of a school evolve, with the goal being to create schools that support engaging and meaningful staff development experiences. Many enthusiastic new teachers learn, often within hours of arriving at their first job, that "in-service days are a waste of time." Given the tendency to have all-consuming meetings during the first few days of each new school year, movement toward meaningful staff development has many challenges to overcome, with the institutional ones among the most challenging.

While moving from current practice to NSES-informed practice is the key challenge, it is helpful to remember that not all change is good; new practices must be assessed to determine their efficacy and their effectiveness. Conscientious and meaningful data collection provides a baseline to assess and evaluate changes brought about by staff development practices. Data collection also serves to support "institutional memory" and provides a reliable history of what has really taken place, as opposed to what participants remember to be the case. Finally, the need to move beyond attendance figures to measure the success of staff development practices is of utmost importance.

Taking all of these issues into consideration, a model of meaningful and effective staff development practices would have the following elements in place:

1. Teacher involvement in all elements of the program and its implementation
2. Meeting the needs of individuals
3. Ensuring a connection between the teacher and the experiences in the teacher's classroom
4. Exploring ideas fully, so that teachers can implement the ideas as conceived
5. Coaching or continual follow-up (Education Place, 1997)

We can see the effectiveness of initiatives such as the TEA when examined through the Education Place framework: all of the elements of meaningful and effective staff development are in practice–along with the participating teacher's commitment to "give back" what was learned by supporting staff development efforts after returning from the Antarctic.

Implications for Practice

Staff development is not simply an ordeal to be endured twice during the semester. Meaningful staff development is designed to change teachers' professional habits and practices. Meaningful staff development is designed to help students learn more effectively and to help teachers become lifelong learners, reaping the benefits of professional growth and, through those professional development experiences, growing personally as well. Professional development helps to build a community within schools and school districts and helps the teacher move from being an isolated individual to being part of a broader professional team.

CLASSROOM SNAPSHOTS

NSES-Informed Professional Development Experiences

Mrs. Blue listened to the crunch of the late autumn leaves on the ground as she made her way across the grounds of the nature center. The scents in the air contrasted nicely with the scents she once associated with professional development meetings held in the auditorium at her high school. Five years had passed since she took part in what some saw as a revolt, but what she and her colleagues felt was an act of professional survival and, ultimately, professional growth. After the last auditorium-bound meeting, Mrs. Blue and a number of her colleagues gathered together and discussed their real needs as science teachers and what it would take to respond to them.

A series of surveys, polls, graduate courses, consultations with the district's staff development administrators, and hard work had led to this most recent success. With the faculty's growing interest in integrating environmental education with their standard science content, the entire science faculty was in the second day of a two-day retreat at a nature center.

What they had created was a conference on issues related to environmental education, with sessions that connected with their own practice in meaningful ways, including issues in assessment, working with agencies beyond the classroom, using GIS technology as a tool in teaching, and many more areas of genuine interest. Other schools in the district were sending their own science teachers to these teacher-generated workshops. K–12 teachers from the entire school district participated. The depth and scope of the institute allowed elementary and middle school teachers to interact with high school teachers, allowing the participants to gain a sense of the multiyear science program in their district that no longer seemed like a series of discrete classroom experiences.

Each of the sessions was organized by members of the science department faculty, with all of them using their recently acquired expertise to share ideas with other faculty members. The institute also boasted some regional and national experts who had been invited to give deep, rich, and meaningful workshops in areas beyond the expertise of the current faculty.

As Mrs. Blue stepped inside the nature center, the conversation among the teachers was far different from the "old days." Conversation about sports and children, which once dominated the between-sessions chatter, had been replaced with enthusiastic discussions of what was learned during the previous session and what they were looking forward to in the following session. Other teachers, according to the survey data gathered the previous day, were already critically examining some of their own teaching practices and were making plans to implement changes immediately. One remark particularly resonated with Mrs. Blue: a teacher confessed her initial disappointment that the institute did not have a "make and take" quality for the sessions, with teachers learning about an activity they could implement the next morning in their classrooms. Rather, she said the experiences she had had would change her entire practice for the rest of her career and she looked forward to the next time a staff development institute would be offered so that her knowledge would continue to grow.

As with previous chapters, the experiences profiled here are not fiction, but are based on the author's observations of meaningful—and well-intentioned but disconnected—staff development practices for teachers. When practices consistent with the National Science Education Standards are used as guidelines for professional development, the movement from disjointed in-service experiences to meaningful professional development parallels the teachers' movement from isolated classroom teachers to professional educators with specialized knowledge and the power to affect their own destiny.

Summary

- Effective staff development practices need to move away from communication of teaching skills and knowledge through large-group lectures, to involve teachers in the conception, the planning, and the delivery of the program.

- Effective staff development programs need to support science teaching practices that promote student-directed inquiry and problem solving, rather than science teaching strategies that emphasize learning science through textbooks and reading.

- Staff development initiatives should seek to combine science knowledge with teaching knowledge, working to support the development of the teacher's pedagogical content knowledge as part of helping teachers appreciate the interrelationship of theory and practice in learning.

- The model of staff development as stand-alone workshops, with neither preparation nor follow-through, needs to be retired and replaced with long-term, enriching experiences for teachers with sufficient coaching and mentoring after the fact so that the goals of the staff development program have some opportunities to succeed.

- Recognizing and applying the expertise of teachers in the staff development process allows schools and school districts to work in collaboration with the district's teachers toward meaningful and widely held staff development goals that support teachers as instructional leaders and not simply as followers.

- Moving beyond the conception of a teacher as merely an individual with technical expertise to a teacher who can use, devise, evaluate, and implement, based on widely varying circumstances, appropriate instructional and curricular approaches.

- Recognizing the teacher as a member of a larger school community, rather than as an individual alone in a classroom, whose professional expertise can benefit the entire instructional community.

- Seeing the teacher as an agent of instructional change, rather than a subject that is the focus of change.

References

American Association for the Advancement of Science. (1989). Science for all Americans. New York: Oxford.

Berliner, D. C. (1985). Knowledge is power. In D. C. Berliner, & B. V. Rosenshine, *Talks to teachers* (pp. 3–33). New York: Random House.

Blank, R. & Hill, S. (2004). Analyzing instructional content and practices. *The Science Teacher, 71*(1), 54–58.

Crave, J. J. (2002). *Teaching teachers: From experts to novices.* Retrieved March 8, 2005, from http://gseweb.harvard.edu/~t656_web/Spring_2002_students/crave_jerad_novice_teacher_learn_from_experts.htm

Danielson, C. (1996). *Enhancing professional practice.* Alexandria, VA: Association for Supervision and Curriculum Development.

Danielson, C. & McGreal, T. L. (2000). *Teacher evaluation to enhance professional practice.* Alexandria, VA: Association for Supervision and Curriculum Development.

Dodge, B. J. (1993). *School-university partnerships and educational technology.* (Eric Document Reproduction Services No. ED 358840)

Education Place. (1997). *Effective staff development.* Retrieved March 9, 2005, from http://www.eduplace.com/rdg/res/literacy/staff_d2.html

Ferraro, J. M. (2000). *Reflective practice and professional development.* (Eric Document Reproduction Services No. ED 449120)

Garmston, R. J. (1998). *Becoming expert teachers.* Retrieved March 8, 2005, from http://www.nsdc.org/library/publications/jsd/garmston191.cfm

Glickman, C. D. (2002). *Leadership for learning: How to help teachers succeed.* Alexandria, VA: Association for Supervision and Curriculum Development.

Hassel, E. (1999). *Professional development.* Oak Brook, IL: North Central Regional Educational Laboratory.

Herr, N. (2001). *Pedagogical content knowledge in science teaching.* Retrieved March 8, 2005, from http://www.csun.edu/~vceed002/ref/pedagogy/pck/

Inhelder, B. & Piaget, J. (1964). *Early growth of logic in the child.* New York: Norton.

National Research Council. (1996). *National science education standards.* National Academy Press: Washington, DC.

National Research Council. (2000). *How people learn.* National Academy Press: Washington, DC.

National Society for the Study of Education. (1957). *Fifty-sixth yearbook: In-service education.* Chicago: University of Chicago Press.

National Society for the Study of Education. (1960). *Fifty-ninth yearbook: Rethinking science education.* Chicago: University of Chicago Press.

Nelson, J. L., Palonsky, S. B., & McCarthy, M. R. (2004). *Critical issues in education.* Boston: McGraw-Hill.

North Central Regional Educational Laboratory. (2004). *Professional development: Learning from the best.* Retrieved March 8, 2005, from http://www.ncrel.org/pd/toolkit.htm

Shulman, L. (1986). Those who understand: Knowledge growth in teachers. *Educational Researcher, 15*(2), 4–14.

Smith, D. C. (2000). Content and pedagogical content knowledge for elementary science teacher educators: Knowing our students. *Journal of Science Teacher Education, 11*(2), 27–46.

Teachers Experiencing Antarctica and the Arctic (2003). *About us.* Available: http://tea.rice.edu/tea_aboutus.html (July 1, 2003).

CHAPTER 8

Putting Principles into Practice

CLASSROOM SNAPSHOTS

Summer "vacation" had just ended for Benjamin, and he was returning home to finish up his preparations for teaching. While one of his colleagues was often heard to mutter that the only good things about teaching were June, July, and August, Benjamin reflected that he often worked harder during the summertime as he prepared for teaching in the fall. This summer was a case in point.

It had been quite a bit different than previous years. Rather than taking graduate classes and developing some instructional units, Benjamin had been accepted into a program in which teachers worked with scientists for the summer at the Department of Natural Resources (DNR). He was inspired to take on this challenge after meeting Betty, a fourth-grade teacher who had spent six weeks in Antarctica conducting research with a geologist; she reported her work to her students.

As a result, he spent the summer working with DNR scientists as a fisheries intern. Some of the work had him assisting biologists with fish sampling, using a number of gear types, and working to identify, measure, and weigh the fish. He was also kept busy recording data and learning firsthand from Steve, the senior biologist, how the data was going to be used to make decisions regarding fish populations over the next few years. With recent controversies over a threatened species of fish and some developing farming practices, decisions were based on making good sense of the data they collected, as they could have a tremendous economic impact throughout the state.

Perhaps it was collecting and using real data all summer that created a flash of memory going back to the time in his science methods course several years before. He recalled being intrigued by the idea of having students really "do" science—and how he had finally "done" science himself, after helping students make sense of it for the last few years. He had made some progress, with students collecting as much real data as possible and using it during their investigations, but the summer's experience had been an epiphany for him.

"This year," he thought, "is going to be really special . . ."

Teaching is an amazing combination of personal and professional skills. As a potential teacher, you've probably been quizzed more than once by teacher education faculty members about why you want to be a teacher. Among your responses, you probably noted your concern for children, an interest in a "giving" profession, or perhaps an interest in the content you would be teaching.

The theme of this book is that the other part of the equation—the professional qualities—can be developed through knowledge and practice. From developing your content knowledge to participating in professional development experiences, the opportunities to grow professionally as a teacher can be enhanced if you know what you should be looking for and what to avoid. The practices advocated in the Standards provide an avenue for improving practice as a science teacher.

As a practicing teacher, you may experience staff development programs similar to the one described at the start of Chapter 7. You will be seated in an auditorium and lectured on what researchers consider the most effective teaching and learning techniques of the present day. You can certainly predict that dry lectures—or even engaging lectures—will not be topping that list of the most meaningful and effective ways to produce meaningful and effective changes in teaching practice.

Regardless of the setting and the topics shared in the vignettes, all of them were based on real teachers engaged in real practices related to teaching, staff development, assessment, and more. Through these narrative experiences I hope that you can now see yourself taking on the role of teacher-as-researcher, teacher-as-staff-developer, and teacher-as-facilitator-of-inquiry.

For those of you currently teaching, I trust that you can see the potential offered by the standards: a tool to liberate, not a set of instructional constraints. In particular, the potentially mind-numbing single-session staff development programs need to be eliminated. Long-term development as a teacher depends on long-term support and the initiative to make it happen for you and your colleagues. The teachers in the opening and closing vignettes took on the challenge of improving staff development and made it a better and more meaningful experience for everyone.

The themes present among the vignettes are quite obviously related to the National Science Education Standards and the perspectives endorsed in the content of these Standards. It is hoped that you learned about the content associated with each of the Standards through the opening vignettes. And as we explored the specific content of each of the Standards in detail, you began to develop an appreciation for how the Standards could be used to support instructional and educational practices that were demonstrated in each chapter's closing vignette. That is the main point of this text.

Another goal of this book has been to assist you in becoming a more informed consumer of information. By alerting you to the most thoughtful and student-centered practices in science teaching, it is hoped that you will look more critically at curricular materials, staff development practices, and assessment activities you encounter. Clearly, you often will be placed in a situation in which you will be assigned a curriculum or other materials and be asked to deliver them to your students. With your science methods course, the practices advocated here, and the National Science Education Standards, there will be opportunities to use many existing high-quality teaching materials, and you can draw out the potential for inquiry in all of them. But the materials themselves do not guarantee effective teaching.

Informing Instructional Practices

The science education standards are exactly that—goals established for all elements of science teaching. Among the most critical of these standards and programmatic goals are the standards associated with instructional practices—the curriculum and instruction related to the teaching of science.

The federal law known widely as No Child Left Behind (NCLB) has had profound effects on the way schools operate. The accountability issues within NCLB have already begun to have an effect on the practices in schools. With respect to the science education standards, it is imperative that teachers know the law, assess students in ways that match what is being taught, and use research-based instructional practices (Yell & Drasgow, 2005).

Teaching the law is beyond the scope of this book, but the points related to ensuring that assessment matches what was taught—and **how** it was taught—informed a considerable part of Chapters 2, 3, and 4 of this text. Ensuring that teachers acquire sound information about student learning requires that the assessment practices they use are aligned with their district's curriculum and with the instruction they deliver in the classroom. With this information in place, teachers can be assured that they are assessing and evaluating what students know, and they can defend their instructional practices.

The final point of using research based practices has been a point of contention in the literature. Without entering the political debate often associated with this discussion, there is abundant research that indicates that effective teachers make a difference in their students' success. Berliner (1987) offers a summary of areas in which educational research supports specific changes in education. He noted over a decade ago that research-based practices on questioning practices, wait time, student grouping, cooperative learning, and curriculum alignment produce results that are both theory-informed and among the key practices to improving teaching and learning in the schools. The practices advocated in the Standards fall into many of those categories, and more. Practices regarding assessment, teacher preparation, curriculum design, and curriculum alignment—all offer important ways to improve instruction. More recently, Gabel's (1994) authoritative **Handbook of Research on Science Teaching and Learning** outlines areas for further investigation in science teaching: how students learn and apply scientific knowledge, the concept of problem solving, the curriculum and the context of the classroom (including school climate, gender issues, and diversity). Again, the purpose of this text is not to examine those issues in detail, but to alert you as a new (or continuing) professional in the field of science teaching that practices evolve and build on prior experiences. What one learns as a new teacher will be refined, enriched, and developed as you continue to grow professionally, especially as you become more conversant in the professional literature that supports science teaching.

Areas of current interest to researchers of teaching science include teaching for conceptual change (to address student misconceptions), how to best examine basic skills in order to develop stronger inquiry-based experiences, and the development and implementation of a spiral-type curriculum that continuously revisits ideas to promote better integration across grade levels and to ultimately increase the student's depth of knowledge. Watch for these as you begin to engage in professional development experiences to see if your in-service practices are based in contemporary research—or whether they are simply taking up your time.

The content associated with science was addressed in the curriculum standards, covering in detail the knowledge that is desired for all students, K–12. The implicit message in the curriculum standards is that science knowledge and skills represent essential knowledge for all students. The content standards further establish that all branches of science—natural and physical—need to be developed in depth at all grade levels. In addition to the development of discrete factual knowledge, the strongest emphasis is on broad conceptual understanding in science that unites the disciplines and connects science with all human experience.

The primary vehicle for connecting the various disciplines of science is a commitment to inquiry-based instructional practices. Chapter 1 of this text laid out the essential elements of classroom inquiry for students. As you recall, inquiry allows considerable flexibility in the way that the teacher allows students to pose questions and solve problems. The teacher will most certainly know what content knowledge he or she wishes to deliver, but allows for the serendipity associated with student-generated questions and curiosity to allow them to follow their own journey to a solution. The teacher in a classroom that embraces inquiry realizes that there can be many possible answers to a question and that valuable meaning can be derived from nearly all of them.

Using inquiry—through student investigation and the generation of questions—as a key instructional tool informs the entire NSES document and the practices it advocates. In essence, the Standards make a strong case for students to learn about science by engaging in science in age-appropriate ways. The underlying belief is that inquiry and scientific modes of thinking and problem-solving can be implemented in a meaningful way for all students at all grade levels.

Developing the use of questioning to support inquiry is an important technique that can be developed by teachers. Work by Carin (1970; Carin & Sund, 1978) observes that most teachers tend to ask convergent questions of their students, with students offering responses that are mainly factual and only demonstrate recall of information. By asking more open-ended and divergent questions, it was shown that teachers can help students offer more diverse responses and increase the involvement of students in classroom discourse. If a teacher were to change any single practice in the classroom based on the reading of this text, a strong case could be argued that using more open-ended questions as a means of engaging more students in inquiry would be a desirable outcome.

Mary Budd Rowe's (1986; 1996) seminal work on the importance of questioning further supports its value in the classroom that supports inquiry. The fast-paced questioning present in many classrooms works against thoughtful discourse; rather, deeper questioning with time for thinking and reflection benefits students in terms of how they think and process information, as well as being more consistent with the goals of student inquiry.

Changing teacher practices represents the means by which inquiry-based practices will become a more common and appropriately implemented classroom strategy. Supporting the movement toward inquiry-based practices must be more effective professional development for teachers. The customary administrator-driven or other "top down" approaches evident in most staff development and in-service programs tend not to support teacher's perceived needs in general and the needs of teachers who teach science in particular. With inquiry as a goal, it is essential that the support teachers receive for their professional practice is consistent with the best contemporary thinking about what that teaching should look like.

Working to match assessment with instruction is an additional challenge offered through the Standards. Having established that our first goal is to teach science through inquiry leads to the recognition that teaching practices must be accompanied by appropriate assessment practices. For assessment to be meaningful, it must be coordinated with the means of instruction used and the content delivered. This presents a singular challenge, as assessing inquiry is profoundly more difficult than assessing discrete content knowledge. Assessing the mastery of discrete content knowledge is relatively simple; assessing how children solve problems and ask and answer their own questions is more difficult by an order of magnitude, yet the rewards of doing this effectively are of equal value. You might want to refer back to the examples on performance-based assessment described in Chapter 3 to see how contemporary assessment practices can be used to assess *how* students are engaged in inquiry.

The Standards as Goals for Improving Instruction

In addition to informing instructional practice, the National Science Education Standards serve as goals for a variety of elements of effective teaching and program development. The Standards do not necessarily tell the reader how to accomplish the content, staff development, or other standards, but instead they recognize that every setting is different, and they identify goals associated with the best thinking about what effective science teaching looks like. The purpose of this book has been to operationalize the Standards and present a picture of what they look like as they are implemented in various schools around the country. How each teacher reaches their goals is unique to the teacher, the school, the school district, and the community, but the consistent theme of innovative instruction, professional development, and performance-based assessment remains present in each of them.

Teaching through inquiry is the main theme of the Standards. All the practices examined throughout this book, and through the Standards as well, were designed to help teachers and instructional systems promote the cause of inquiry in science teaching. Whether it be improving assessment practices, addressing the needs of science education systems, or promoting more thoughtful professional development, the theme of inquiry remains the core experience that everything else is designed to support.

The Standards provide tools to help teachers think about what qualifies as "effective science learning." Both content knowledge and the ability to conduct independent inquiry provide core experiences. The Standards, with a commitment to thinking skills and content knowledge, remind teachers that there are multiple "ways of knowing" and that engaging in inquiry can help more students more effectively construct their own knowledge and thus better assimilate and accommodate that knowledge as they build on it over time.

The Standards also promote staff development as a means of improving instruction. However, the staff development envisioned in the Standards is a process that involves the teachers as participants throughout the entire process, and not just as recipients of information that others have determined to be of value. Teachers must have a role in the planning, implementation, and assessment of staff development programs; they must not be content to simply receive information.

When staff development is addressed in concert with curriculum development and coordinating science experiences throughout the entire curriculum and among various stakeholders in teacher preparation, the role of teachers as key players in the entire science education system becomes essential. Only then will the changes that are necessary to support science education become systemic.

Educational Change

If one looks at the language of change, it is nearly always referred to as "dealing with change." Clearly, the message is that change presents problems for us to contend with. Participating in change is a challenge faced by all human beings. Both professional and popular literature abound with information and strategies designed to help people cope with changes in their personal and professional lives. A book with the unlikely title **Who Moved My Cheese**? (Johnson, 1998) became a best seller as it sought to help individuals deal with the pervasive nature of change. Clearly, most people do not enjoy change, do not seek out change, and resist change when it is forced upon them.

As a teacher, you will likely enter a school that is moving toward the practices described in this book. Some of your colleagues will be leading the charge to promote change. Some will resist it, and some will mutter cynically, "We've seen all this before." I submit that this last sentiment does not accurately reflect the case.

Educational change in science education historically has not been focused on making such large-scale *systemic* changes to science education systems. Most change advocated during the last forty years has focused on either one of two issues: improving the curriculum or improving the teacher. The curriculum programs of the 1960s underscored the curriculum development approach; the staff development initiatives of the 1980s and the 1990s represented the second perspective.

The goal of the Standards, however, is to produce changes throughout the entire science education system, not just improving teachers' skills and developing and using sound curriculum. It includes not only thinking deeply about the science curriculum and helping teachers through staff development, but also on developing teachers as experts in their own professional development and as agents for instructional improvement across the entire breadth and scope of the science education system. It is my hope, both as a teacher and as the author of this text, that as you have read each chapter, you have reflected on the nature of effective science teaching, the nature of quality staff development, the value of the content standards, and the need to work with your colleagues as a teacher and as a learner—fully expecting your skills as a teacher to evolve.

None of the stories shared here happened overnight—or, in some cases, a single year. Educational change is difficult, but it takes place because teachers value their students and their role as a teacher. Across the school curriculum, science offers among the best opportunities to promote not only a body of fascinating knowledge, but also a set of powerful thinking skills that cross all boundaries of the curriculum.

CLASSROOM SNAPSHOTS

Looking Back . . . and Looking Ahead

Four years into her professional life as a teacher, Jennifer's mother gave her a box full of memorabilia from her childhood. The mementos in the box, some well over twenty years old, brought back a flood of memories, particularly of the "teaching" she delivered to the stuffed animals and dolls she found in the box. The wash of memories related to her teaching practice included more recent history as well—the close of her student teaching experiences.

During her student teaching internship, her university supervisor was also her science methods instructor, Professor Rojo. Besides challenging her during her science methods course, he also inspired her to teach science through inquiry. This was a major shift in her concept of teaching. She had always imagined that teaching was something you did to students, rather than something you might learn with students.

She was able to take this farther during her student teaching experiences. During the spring semester, her school had historically participated in a science fair. Her cooperating teacher assigned her the responsibility of working with students as they developed their science fair projects and coordinating the judging.

This sort of experience was very different from the large-group, direct instruction Jennifer had experienced during many of her college classes. She had twenty-eight fifth grade students, at a variety of ability levels and with a variety of levels of interest, many of them uninterested in participating in a science fair. She expressed her frustration and concern to Dr. Rojo.

Because of her discussion with Dr. Rojo, what Jennifer originally perceived as a frightful problem was recast as an opportunity. The chance to work with students as they conducted their own inquiry was presented as a great opportunity to apply the ideas developed during the science methods course. For the students, the questions would be real—something they had a genuine interest in and a curiosity to satisfy. For her, the opportunity to help students ask and answer their own questions would give her the chance to implement the science teaching she had come to value.

Ultimately, the value of what Jennifer was attempting to do was externally validated as three of her students—a school record—made it to the school district competition, and one of the three made it to the state science fair conference. Jennifer's task was not easy. While students carried out investigations in diverse disciplines, such as plants and properties of matter, Jennifer was required to learn this content with her students. But despite the professional challenges required, it was abundantly clear that all of her students learned a great deal, not just the "winners."

Jennifer received further external validation as the principal and a group of teachers at her school asked her to present a "how to" session during an upcoming staff development program. Her final measure of success came as she was encouraged to apply for an opening at the school where she did her student teaching. At the end of the spring semester, she graduated and had a job waiting for her in the fall.

Jennifer is still growing professionally as a teacher, and she continues what she began as a student teacher—sharing her experiences with her colleagues at staff development programs. Lately, she has presented workshops at venues such as her state science teachers' conference.

Jennifer's experiences chart the growth of a teacher whose practice is consistent with the goals espoused by the National Science Education Standards. She was a participant in her own professional development and that of others, and she focused on inquiry as the key experience for her students. If we could follow her further, we might expect to see her taking a leadership role in curriculum development within her school district and pursuing further professional development through a graduate degree.

None of this happens all at once, but meaningfully constructed experiences work together not only to improve one's ability to teach, but also to expand opportunities for students to learn—and for teachers to learn with them. May good teaching—and its companion, good learning—be always with you.

References

Berliner, D. C. (1987). Knowledge is power. In D. C. Berliner & B. V. Rosenshine (Eds.), *Talks to teachers* (pp. 1–33). New York: Random House.

Carin, A. A. (1970). Techniques for developing discovery questions. *Science and Children, 7*(7), 13–15.

Carin, A. A. & Sund, R. B. (1978). *Creative questioning and sensitive listening techniques: A self-guided approach.* Upper Saddle River, NJ: Merrill.

Gabel, D. L. (1994). *Handbook of research on science teaching and learning.* New York: Macmillan.

Johnson, S. (1998). *Who moved my cheese.?* New York: Putnam.

Rowe, M. B. (1986). Wait times: Slowing down may be a way of speeding up. *Journal of Teacher Education, 37*(1), 43–50.

Rowe, M. B. (1996). Science, silence, and sanctions. *Science and Children, 34*(1), 35–37.

Yell, M. L. & Dragow, E. (2005). *No child left behind: A guide for professionals.* Upper Saddle River, NJ: Pearson.

Index

DATE DUE
